Bite of the Travel Bug

Galavanting Goddess
Chronicles of a life well lived

Lisa Ruoff

Copyright © 2023 by Lisa Ruoff

All rights reserved. This book or any portion thereof may not be reproduced or used in any manner whatsoever without the express written permission of the publisher except for the use of brief quotations in a book review.
Any resemblance to persons living or dead should be plainly apparent to them and those who know them, especially if the author has been kind enough to have provided their real names. All events described herein actually happened, are true, and written down to the best of the author's memory and ability.

Printed in the United States of America
First Printing 2023

ISBN 978-1-7370494-2-5 paperback
ISBN 978-1-7370494-3-2 ebook

Published by Lisa Ruoff LLC
231 Durango Rd, Durango CO
81301 www.lisaruoff.com

Also by Lisa Ruoff:

Galavanting Goddess: Alaska to Cuba and Back

Introduction

"A girl should be two things: who and what she wants."
- Coco Chanel

Even as a young child, I never fit the profile of normal. As the youngest of six kids, and the fifth girl of those six, I always knew there was something inherently "not-right" about me. And at the time, there was no "sassy is strong in a daughter" kind of talk. Being sassy just meant I was a downright pain in the ass! It also meant that I was grounded a lot.

I was a troublemaker, a rabble-rouser. Not that I meant to make trouble or rouse rabbles, so to speak. I simply wasn't content with being the good girl. The girl who was seen but never heard. The girl who did as she was told and didn't ask questions. The girl who settled for what life gave her. Nope. Not me. I always wanted more.

Not only did I want answers, but I never stopped asking questions. "Why?" was not just a phase for me, or if it was, I'm still in that phase now at 51 years of age. My mother was not one to nourish my differentness. It only made her tired and frustrated. Me being me made her tired and frustrated. She had already raised five kids and now THIS?! I mean, at one point, I etched the words "I HATE MOM" in my wooden desk with a pencil. How's that for persistence and pain-in-the-ass-ness?

And it's not like I had it bad. I never needed for necessities. We always had lots of food in the house. I grew amphibious every summer when the pool in the backyard became my domain. I had to walk through the hot tub room to get to the TV room. Really, my parents did not leave us wanting for material things. Yes, I had that streak in me. I needed to know WHY I wasn't supposed to date my black friend, Mike (remember, that was the 80's and I was the last of six kids. My parents were still of a certain era back then).
Or WHY I couldn't go hang out with my friends until 2am (could pregnancy not occur unless it was after midnight?). Or WHY alcohol was supposed to be bad for me when I saw all the adults around me drinking.

A few of my other siblings had made their way out of the nest by going overseas in high school as exchange students to foreign countries. Of course, my grades weren't good enough to do that – being the bad girl doesn't lend to getting good grades. I tried to play by the rules. At least in my mind I did. But I just couldn't pull off the charade. And by the second year of college, I packed up my little two-seater Honda CRX and hit the road to "visit" my sister in Colorado. When my mother saw the microwave in the passenger seat, I'm pretty sure she surmised my lack of intent to return. And, really, there must have been a level of relief there for her. There had to be a little voice in her head that said, "See ya!", followed by a big, heavy sigh. Not that she would ever admit that, but I wouldn't blame you, Mom.

Most of my young life, I was jokingly called "the mistake." As the story goes, my parents had been trying for another child, the sixth, for a few years with no luck. Giving up on what her body had to offer, my mother went the way of adoption. Mom and Dad were turned down by numerous organizations because they already had five children. (This never made much sense to me, but I guess times were different then.) Then, at last, an agency found them to be acceptable parents for a brother and a sister from another country.

Just about the time my parents received this happy news, my mom learned she was pregnant with me. Hence, the mistake. Over the years, the mistake took on a meaning of its own due to my firecracker, bull-headed disposition, let's say. I didn't even realize my moniker could be interpreted as derogatory until friends in high school were appalled by the term! It was a kind of point of pride for me, really, being the mistake.

I resolved to reframe the context of my somewhat dismal nickname. Proudly, I called myself "the prodigy child." Even though everyone else might have thought of me as a mistake, which, technically, may have been correct since I wasn't exactly planned, I knew I wasn't! Maybe it was my first act of defiance. My way of making my grand entrance, against the all-knowing words of my mothers' pompous doctors (all male, of course). Here I am – take that! Although my newly-revised title of "prodigy child" never quite took off with the rest of the family, it nestled down inside of me and became part of who I am.

As a female child of the 70's, I was not once told that my willfulness was an asset. That was only accepted in boys. Us girls were supposed to be "broken" of that kind of unacceptable behavior. Women's empowerment, or girl power, was not a thing at that time. At least not in my family in southern New Jersey. It wasn't until I had experienced some of life and realized, on my own, that stubborn pigheadedness can actually be essential for a single woman trying to make something of herself.

Finding a man to take care of me never interested me. And I certainly didn't fit the mold of the good girl who finds Mr. Right, gets married, ends up with 2.5 kids, a white picket fence, and a mini-van somewhere in suburbia. Even before I knew that was an option, it wasn't in my DNA. I was wired differently. And by differently, I was beginning to understand that wasn't a bad thing. My differences were what made me an individual. ESPECIALLY as a woman, not in spite of being a woman. Those young years in Colorado taught me a lot about myself. But I was about to find out a whole lot more!

My staunch independence began way before my solo backpacking trip across the world. But that adventure only fanned the flames of what had been lying dormant since my childhood. Being a strong woman doesn't come easily in a world like mine. I had to fight like hell and had to believe in myself when I seemingly had no one – and particularly no woman – to guide me.

Guaranteed, every powerful woman has at least one distinguishing, colorful story of how she became who she is. Stories of hardship, sorrow, pain, heartache, determination, strength, resourcefulness, resilience, courage, intelligence, patience, and stamina. Stories that only other kindred spirits can relate to. In my own world, it was solo traveling in my younger years, and then immersing myself into a cut-throat, high-stakes, male-dominated field as a female chef, an experience I'll recount in a future book. Stay tuned.

In our so-called modern world, dichotomies abound between accepted feminine and masculine traits. Women who are outspoken and headstrong are seen as bossy and mouthy while men with these characteristics are considered leaders. Men are expected to punt the child-rearing and housekeeping to their wives. Somehow, we women are expected to manage a career and the domestic life of our families, or our "performance" is inadequate and we are considered inferior, with no acknowledgement that being a wife, mother, and manager of the home is among the most difficult jobs known to humankind. I remember, in my adult years, one of my male friends commented on how great it was that his buddy, a new father, helped his wife so much around the house. The enlightened spouse's retort was absolutely perfect, and heartfelt:

"I live here, too. This is my baby, too. I'm not 'helping her out.' I'm just doing my share of the chores." An absolutely perfect response to a ludicrous societal assessment regarding the division of labor. If only all men shared his view.

President John F. Kennedy signed the Equal Pay Act into law in 1963. This Act prohibits gender-based wage discrimination for people performing jobs that require substantially equal skill, effort, and responsibility under similar working conditions. Fast forward nearly 60 years. We have women in the White House, on the Supreme Court, running Fortune 500 companies, in outer space. And yet, this law is broken every single day. Women still do not receive equal pay, even for exactly the same position.

As a female chef, I had to work ten times as hard as any male chef I ever knew in order to receive barely equal treatment. And even then, it was a hard sell. Why?

Because I had breasts and a vagina. The downside to being a strong, powerful, independent woman is that it took me until I was fifty years old to marry someone who had balls as big as mine! But I'm jumping ahead of myself...

> *"If you don't like the road you're walking, start paving another one."*
> *- Dolly Parton*

Fast forward to a few years after my cross-country trip with microwave as my co-pilot. After two of my four obligatory college years, I dropped out and became a bartender. By then, I was fully into party mode and there was no going back! Colorado life fit me like a cashmere glove on a Vermont winter's night, and I was home. But even my fun-filled, drug-enhanced, sex-ridden Colorado days started to become mundane.

There was one night, hanging with my (so-called) ex-convict friends, in their short-term rental room in a shitty, run-down motel called The Rex (creatively unique, huh?). We were all stoned out of our minds; I looked down and there was a 9mm handgun sitting in my lap. There was some such discussion of how awesome it was, and all I could think was, "I gotta get the fuck outta here. This path has got to change." And that night things shifted for me. Not that I stopped partying, but I did give myself a hard enough kick in the ass to get out of the gutter I'd fallen into. It took a bit, but I made some more substantial emotional connections, aka friends, in my life, and quit the bartending and waitressing scene. Got myself a real job, managing the office of a green building supply business in town.

There was a time, as office manager in that cute little Colorado mountain town, that none of it was filling me up. It wasn't enough. And there was no reason why. I just knew I had to go. It was the feeling of driving to work in the morning and not wanting to take that turn to the office. "Just keep going," my mind kept saying. And not stopping until I've made it to the other side of the country. Or, better yet, driving to the airport and leaving everything behind to fly off to some exotic destination.

The year was 1995. I was twenty-three years young. I had no money. And I had to go. Leave it all behind and just go. I didn't go in such an expedient or dramatic fashion as to ditch my car at the American Airlines curbside check-in. But go, I did! Those months of travel changed the course of my adult life, causing it to shift lanes and direction.

My family had gone on numerous international trips when I was a kid, and I joined them on a few. It's not like leaving the country was new to me. But leaving the country on my own, as a single female traveler definitely was. It added a whole new light to traveling. A light that would never be dimmed, from that day forward. Even decades later, this book was written in different parts of the Mexican highlands while traipsing around and "working" on my writing for a few months, as well as a guesthouse on the beach in Jamaica. Vermont, Colorado, and New Jersey were included in that list, as well, but they lack the flair for the exotic.

> *"Though I didn't realize it at the time, it wasn't who's going to let me, but who's going to stop me?"*
> *- Anais Nin*

The Galavanting Goddess Chronicles were born because friends encouraged me to share my adventures which they found unusual, informative, and highly entertaining. Also, they felt it particularly important because I was recounting a significant chapter of my life that took place 25 years ago. Consequently, I was capturing social, economic, political, humanitarian, and environmental nuggets of history in a manner that was educational and vibrant, brimming with the enthusiasm, and sometimes naïveté, of youth.

    Some of the points they made had never occurred to me, and I decided to follow their guidance. In doing so, I realized how empowering both my external and internal journeys have been for me and learned that people were genuinely interested in knowing more.

A few decades later I was compelled to move to Vermont. I had been offered a job as an executive chef, with a specific focus of turning the kitchen all organic, at a small but busy restaurant in Burlington. Even though I loved my Rocky Mountains, I felt that I needed a change. There was that stinking travel bug at work again.

My upcoming relocation to the Northeast was drawing near, and I was excited yet a bit trepidatious about leaving behind my beloved mountains. My friend, Jim, who had spent many years of his life in the Adirondack mountains of NY not far from Vermont, made a comment about the move that confounded me.

"People there will find you very interesting," was his exact terminology. Huh? I found that an intriguing and confusing statement until a few years later.

After renovating my 200-year-old farmhouse in Vermont, I taught cooking classes from my pastoral kitchen. One of my participants was a woman from Boston who was asking me about my past and how I had ended up in Vermont. After briefly explaining about my time in Alaska, Colorado, and then buying a historic brick farmhouse on an island in the middle of Lake Champlain (I didn't even get into the international stuff!) and turning it into a Bed & Breakfast, she turned to me with a very bewildered and almost envious look and stated, in a matter-of-fact kind of way,

"Wow. You are a very interesting woman!"

Ah, Jim, it's all clear to me now...

The how, why, when, and where seemed to intrigue people. Hence, I have come to see these chronicles as a map of my process of personal blooming, documenting growth and awareness of my experiences – some humorous, some poignant, some alarming, any or all of which might, at the very least, be amusing and entertaining. Then again, maybe these pages will inspire or motivate a confused and scared young woman looking for her next step; or that middle-aged woman who is finally taking her chances at living those dreams she never thought she could make real.

> *"I'd rather regret the things I've done than regret the things I haven't done."*
> *- Lucille Ball*

There's something about travel that ignites the soul. Something about being stripped of your comfort zone in a foreign land. Having your first-world privilege shockingly shoved in your face while experiencing third-world poverty. Understanding, maybe for the first time in your life, what it feels like to be a minority when you find your white skin stands out like a shining beacon among throngs of beautiful shades of black-brown bodies. Being thrown into a situation where your native tongue falls on deaf ears. Not knowing the currency or what is expected of money etiquette (Do I tip? Do I haggle? Do I bribe the police?). Or better yet, having no money and having to figure it out in a completely foreign financial world. Being utterly uncomfortable in your own skin. Being forced into absolute vulnerability and relying solely on trust and intuition. There is no learning curve in the world that is so disquieting and so worth going through. DAMN, it's completely invigorating! This feeling, when you allow yourself to be in the place for it to happen, is what they call being bitten by the travel bug. That complete, utter, luxurious, terrifying, insufferable, thoroughly explicitly resplendent bite of the travel bug. Once bitten, just give in – there is no cure. Nor will you ever want one.

"Certainly, travel is more than the seeing of sights; it is a change that goes on, deep and permanent, in the ideas of living."
–Mary Ritter Beard

Lisa Ruoff

Australia

"Don't worry about the world ending today. It's already tomorrow in Australia." -Charles Schulz

Although there were tears streaming down my cheeks, I would have been hard pressed to find a soul on the planet who would have felt sorry for me at that moment. There I was, watching the sun rise over the famed white sands of the Australian east coast, somewhere near Sydney. It was too early for the long stretch of white sandy beach to have many visitors. Only a few hardy souls were in sight. It should have been a beautiful event. But, instead of reveling in the glory of a new day, I couldn't stop crying. I felt completely out of sorts – lonely, isolated, and scared, in unfamiliar territory. This was my first international excursion on my own. Completely solo. I wasn't even sure where I was. Just that the taxi driver dropped me off at a backpackers' hostel near the beach. What beach? I couldn't have told you. It didn't matter to me, though. My location or my surroundings wouldn't have made a difference. I had no foundation, no security blanket, no safety zone… It was like I was floating around in space with no connection to ground control, and it totally freaked me out. The newness and rawness of my self-inflicted solo status were overwhelming. And I was terrified.

My flight to Sydney from Denver landed during the wee hours of the morning. I jumped in the first taxi I could find and headed for the nearest backpackers' hostel the driver knew of. My plan was to get to the hostel, check in, dump my stuff somewhere safe, and then explore my whereabouts. But when I arrived, it was not yet sunrise, way too early to check in. So, I carted my tired, overloaded, bewildered ass over to the beach, which wasn't far from the hostel.

Having completely over-packed, every time I tried to put on my backpack, I found myself upended like a turtle – flat on my back on top of the pack, my feet and arms helplessly flailing about. At the airport, I provided free entertainment for travelers who pretended not to see me as I struggled to right myself under the monstrosity of my shell. Now, I was on the beach. Nesting ground of the sea turtle. My inability to emotionally right myself further wounded my pride and made me feel inept. It was an apt metaphor for my upside-down life and my sense of powerlessness in that moment. The irony of the situation blatantly smacked me upside the head.

As the sun rose and illuminated my surroundings, I sat hunched over in the sand, holding my knees tight to my chest, feeling immensely sorry for my miserable self. The turtle seeking refuge and protection in its shell.

I cried and cried. Earlier I had tried to call my sister, Lynn, to no avail. No answer. Damn the time difference, which I was going to have to adjust to if I wanted to speak to anyone anywhere any time soon.

I missed Warren and would have given anything to have him next to me, our toes in the sand, enjoying the moment as it should have been enjoyed, sharing the beginning of a new adventure with the man I loved. There was no way to get in touch with him, either. I was left with no choice but to sit with my emotions, desolate, on a stunningly beautiful and pristine beach.

About an hour into my pity party, I got real. I did this. I chose to be here, by myself, on another continent far, far away. It was my choice to leave my comfortable life in Colorado and my boyfriend of two years. Yes, it was all my choice.

What happened to my excitement? What the hell was I crying about? Why was I feeling so sorry for myself? My first morning on that stunning Australian beach, I experienced near physical and emotional paralysis because I was so far removed from all that was familiar to me. As Neil Donald Walsch so perfectly sums it up, "Life begins at the end of your comfort zone." That morning was the beginning of my life's transformation. Since that time, being out of my comfort zone has become my comfort zone!

But at that moment, I made the decision to take a deep breath, push through my fear, be fully present, and engage in this once-in-a-lifetime experience. To be fully present, I had to allow myself to truly feel and embrace the fear, unease, and discomfort that wracked me. There was no way around it, only through.

I sat silently on the cool sand and closed my eyes. I let the fine granules of millions of miniscule shells sift through my fingers and asked the Earth for guidance. I asked the Ocean for wisdom and stability. And I asked my Angels for the ability to see joy in all things. And, you know what? It worked! As usual, the Elements heard my prayers and delivered.

After a while, I opened my eyes – now dry – and the beauty of my surroundings slowly seeped into my soul. I had gotten myself this far, and it was time to begin my adventure. My journey "down under" that would shape the journey within.

How had I chosen this place? What made me decide to pack my life into that ill-fitting beast of a backpack? To chuck it all and go? It had started a month or so before, while I was living in Colorado. I got bit by the bug. And that damned bug will not be denied. I held it at bay for a bit, but it kept coming at me, torturing me with its incessant buzz, like a voracious mosquito. I understood what it meant to feel like I was crawling out of my skin.

Driving to work in the morning had become a lesson in restraint. All I wanted to do was keep on driving and not make that turn into the office, even though it was a small office with great friends and surrounded by Rocky Mountain splendor in a cute, little, outdoorsy town. None of that seemed to matter. I had reached the point where I could no longer fight it. The all-consuming thoughts of new sights, new sounds, beckoned me. Like others before me, I just had to DO something and GO somewhere. It really was out of my hands.

I didn't have a specific place in mind, so I chose my destination the good, old-fashioned way. I pulled out my sister's World Atlas, that voluptuous publication of the entire globe with full-page glossy, sexy pages in vivid color. The atlas really was quite a carnal pleasure for me at times!

I closed my eyes, randomly opened that enticing, lascivious book to a page, and put my finger down on a spot. When I opened my eyes, that right index finger was smackdab in the middle of the continent of Australia. That was it. That was my destination. The great land of Oz. The land of numerous poisonous, wild creatures, and five time zones.

It wasn't quite as simple as just buying a ticket and getting on a plane, though. For starters, despite hiccups, I happened to be in a pretty serious relationship with my boyfriend, Warren. I had stuff: furniture, two cats, a car, a job, though I didn't really have any money. But you cannot say "no" to the travel bug. After much thought and consideration (okay, not really that much thought or consideration), I started the wheels in motion.

Warren and I had been doing this on-and-off thing for a while. We were both young and carefree and though we loved each other, neither of us was ready to be "pinned down." We considered traveling together, but he'd been globe-trotting for several years and was planning to return to his homeland of South Africa to see what life there might hold for him. We mutually decided that we needed to do what felt right for us individually, and we hoped in the long run, we would meet up again and continue our path together.

I told myself it was time to see what this relationship was made of. My need to travel really had nothing to do with him or us. I would have loved for us to be travel partners, and to have those shared experiences, but more so, I had to fulfill this urge, with or without him. World traveler that he was, he understood. We even discussed the possibility of me continuing on to South Africa after my Australia adventures. Anything was possible…. But it was too far away for either of us to make any concrete plans. For the moment, Australia was the focus. And it was gonna be me, solo.

Lisa Ruoff

My roommate, Amy, and I decided it was best to find new homes for our two cats, Shadow and Sage. We found a wonderful home for Shadow with a little girl who immediately fell in love with her. Sage had simply shown up at the window one night and never left. We both thought she was going to be the easy one to place because she was still a kitten (or so we thought because of her tiny size). But that little harlot threw us quite an unexpected curveball. One night, in the early stages of executing the "Escape to Australia" plan, Amy called me at work.

"It seems that we are grandparents," she announced cryptically over the phone.

She went on to explain that our cute little orphan kitty had crawled into the safety of the stovetop – that's how small she was – to deliver four of the cutest fuzzballs you've ever seen. Amy had to take apart the stovetop to determine why the kitty wasn't coming out, and BAM! There Mama and babies were! We didn't even know Sage was pregnant. Now we had four little cuties and a mama who couldn't be separated from them for at least eight weeks.

We were about two weeks away from having to vacate the apartment and stumped on what to do. Thank God for sisters! Lynn came to my rescue. Her hubby, Art, was not crazy about the idea of welcoming the feline family, but I convinced him it was just until the kittens could be weaned and then they could all find good homes.

When I returned from Oz, six months later, Art and the Sage kitty were besties and he had cut a hole in the back wall as a cat door for her. That one-and-the-same little harlot kitty never grew bigger than a kitten due to her young pregnancy. Sage stayed with my sister until the day she died, at twenty years old. That's 96-years old in human years. Not a bad gig for the freeloading, pregnant vagabond who showed up at the window one night!

And then there was all the stuff – furniture, household goods, my Jeep. As it turned out, selling most of it made me enough money to feel secure in traveling for at least a few months without having to work. The Jeep brought in the biggest chunk. Praises be! Besides the money, another great advantage of selling everything I owned is that I didn't have to pay for storage. Bonus. I was able to leave a few bags of personal belongings with Lynn and Art for safe keeping. It was helpful to have someone close who was stable and secure (which is an extremely ironic statement to make because later in life those tables would turn in the extreme).

I would have given anything to have all of that back again as I sat on that beach. Not only Warren, but the stuff, the cats, the jeep, the job, too. I was regretting every aspect of my decision. Most of all, I just wanted a friend to be there with me. I missed Warren. And I missed my sister. I was clueless as to what I was doing, or where I was going, or why I was even there in the first place. What the actual fuck had I been thinking?!

My heart yearned for Warren. It felt like a quick fix to my fear and unease in that moment to just lean my head on his shoulder and have him play with my hair. My mind was screaming at me, "WHY?"

"Why did you leave him? What is wrong with you?!"

It had only been about two years, which is nothing in the span of a lifetime. But it was a very intense and intimate two years. It was, as I would find out, a two-year period that would steer the course of my relationships for the next 30 years.

I was tending bar the night he came in with a friend. They sat in a booth near the bar. When I took their order, I couldn't help but be besotted with his gorgeous blue eyes, which seemed to see straight into my soul, and his thick, unkempt, wavy blond hair. But then he spoke and that accent. Oh, I was a goner! I'm a total sucker for accents, and his South African lilt did me in. On the outside, I might have been wearing my bartending-warrior-shield (similar to standing bitch face, but necessary to hold a power position as a female in a house of inebriation). On the inside, I was all mush.

Coffee was his drink of choice that evening; I was able to let my bartending-warrior-shield down a bit and flirt some, subtly, of course. I must have gone to his table at least twenty times in those few hours to refill his cup (real subtle, right?). I'm not really sure if he was actually capable of drinking that much coffee, or if he was just as enamored with me as I was with him and wanted me to be near him. I chose to believe the latter.

After my shift, we sat there for hours, drinking more coffee, and alternately chatting about topics big and small. We brainstormed and strategized on how to save the planet from our species and their foibles. And that was that. We were together from that night forward. He was living at the hostel in Glenwood Springs, and I was living in my sister's basement, and it took us all of about fifteen minutes to move in together.

For the next two years, we took impromptu overnight road trips to the Canyonlands of Utah, camped out under the stars in the backcountry of Colorado's Rocky Mountains, attempted to become parents of a crazy, beautiful, killer husky (which didn't end well for a local flock of Canadian geese. Sorry…), ate lots of mushrooms, dropped more than a few tabs of acid, smoked a shit ton of pot, and drank enormous amounts of alcohol throughout it all.

We couldn't keep our hands and lips off each other. He was unlike any lover I had had. It was so much more than great sex; it was possibly the first time in my life that I experienced making love. And we lavishly partook of that passionate, most intimate, and beautiful human connection just about everywhere and just about all the time!

Our reverence for nature was part of our bond. We each loved to be outdoors and spent as much time there as we could, having fun and recharging our bodies and souls. Our preferred activities included whitewater rafting, tubing down rivers, hiking, snowboarding, or four-wheeling in the backcountry in search of perfect camping sites. And there was that month or so that we took a road trip in my open-topped Jeep out to the West Coast. The infamous and absolutely unforgettable trip that almost was the "trip that wasn't" due to one of those rare, but unfortunate, events. It happened our first night on the road.

It was about midnight; we had made it all the way past Salt Lake City and were feeling pretty much indomitable on our quest to the Pacific Northwest. With approximately six hours under our belts, and almost twelve in front of us, we figured we'd find a hidden little pull-off somewhere on National Forest land and set up camp for at least a few hours of shut-eye. I was driving, and Warren was riding shotgun, half-asleep, when we suddenly smelled smoke. After a few distraught and hectic minutes of searching, we finally realized the source was somewhere behind the driver's seat.
What the hell?!

I pulled over quickly, and we both jumped out and started rummaging through the back of the Jeep, throwing things onto the side of the road haphazardly in search of the source of smoke. It only took a minute to pinpoint my purse that was stashed under the seat, and which happened to be smoldering! Every smoker's nightmare: tossing a cigarette butt that boomerangs back into the car and catches fire. The top was down, but the wind was coming from the wrong direction. Into the back seat the butt stealthily flew, landing on top of my cloth purse, which was the repository for the big wad of cash that was to bankroll our adventure.

That big wad of cash, which was folded in half, was burnt right down the middle of the folded bundle. HOLY SHIT! Our money for the month up in smoke! So, there I was at midnight on the side of the road in the middle of nowhere, just west of Salt Lake City, having a meltdown over our catastrophic loss. We had no credit card. No backup. The charred cash was it. Oh, dear Jesus! I was a mess, crying and screaming at the heavens. All Warren could do was try to console me, without success. We had worked hard for that money and were so excited for our month ahead.

"Now what?" we asked each other, in a state of shock. We decided to continue with our plan to crash for the night at a decent Forest pull-off, and head for the nearest town in the morning, find a bank, and see if we could somehow salvage at least some of the cash.

Morning came. Not very optimistically, we went to the bank. One very surprised and confused teller stared at us, mouth agape, as we held out to him two small bundles of burnt, crispy cash. We learned that fine morning that there are two identical serial numbers on each paper bill. Miraculously, our wad of cash burned exactly down the middle; all the individual dollars had both serial numbers intact. The bank replaced all of our money. Every. Single. Last. Dollar.

How's THAT for the Universe looking out for us?!!! Shit like that happened to us all the time. Things that seemed to be unlucky always resolved in our favor, and we began to feel just a bit magical in our partnership. Should we have interpreted our good fortune as a sign that we should stop smoking? Perhaps. But in our youth-induced egotistical naïveté, we didn't even consider smoking cessation. At least for a few more years, anyway.

After our miraculous gift, we continued our drive to the coast, feeling somewhat invincible. We camped in hidden, vacant spaces and were lucky enough not to get caught. We ran joyously on the beaches of the Pacific Northwest and bathed naked in remote hot springs of the Oregon forests. No matter where we were, being outdoors and connected to our natural setting was intensely satisfying, physically, emotionally, and spiritually.

When we returned to Colorado, on one of our outings we had to hunker down in our tent in the middle of the afternoon due to a huge, sudden oncoming storm. Black clouds descended upon us in a fury; thunder and lightning assaulted our eyes and ears. The wind buffeted the huge conifers surrounding us, almost doubling them over. We thought for sure they would break and come crashing down on our small, inconsequential shelter. And yet, I felt completely safe huddled up with him in our sleeping bags. We looked out in awe at the force and power of nature surrounding us yet felt invincible in each other's arms. That storm was a gift. Our own personal show. And we reveled in every second of its furious beauty, together.

Everything between us was intimate. There was absolutely nothing superficial in our relating to one another during those years. It was all straight to the core. It was wondrous. And allowing myself to be that close to another human being was probably the scariest thing I'd ever done.

He was my soulmate (whatever that meant in my early twenties), and I was his – or so I believed. I adored his South African accent, and his long, thick, curly blonde hair. Surprisingly, I didn't mind that he wasn't tall. Being about the same height made it that much easier to stare deeply into each other's soul.

He wasn't quite the romantic type, not in the standard sense of romance. He wasn't the kind of guy to send me roses. But wildflowers, freshly picked and delivered with a prolonged hug and tender kiss – that was more his style. Or fresh strawberries sliced open and rubbed across my lips so I might savor their pure Spring-ness – much better than roses! He won me over, heart and soul. He was so real. There was no bullshit. Just pure honesty, love, and connection. It was unnerving at times, but my soul craved his realness. He entranced me. And, in fact, we bewitched each other. For a while.

Though we agreed to go our own ways, we believed we had the quintessential romance that would have the quintessential happy ending. That was our plan, the happy ending. When the wanderlust bug bit me, our timing slipped. Our connection, our future had been thrown to the winds of fate. I had done that. And I was deeply regretting my decision while sitting on that stretch of brilliant Australian sand that morning.

But I had to live with my decision. I had to pull myself together. I had to trust that it would all turn out exactly as it needed to be. And by the time I headed back to the hostel, I had gotten my head screwed on straight again. Big, deep breaths, lots of motivational talk, and I had my game face on by the time I walked through the door.

Staying at hostels is a great way to avoid being alone. And being around people helped me find my way back to the light and out of my self-wallowing cave. Within a few days, I was meeting lots of foreign travelers and finding out a ton of information about where to go and what to do while I was in the glorious land of "down under." The demographic of clientele at hostels was almost always other backpackers, mostly in their twenties, who were also great conversationalists in times of need. Almost all travelers can understand the emotional highs and lows while being so far away from home. An empathetic ear was never far when my alter ego, self-pity, arrived for a visit.

The random selection made by my index finger did not disappoint. Australia was downright amazing! Those first few weeks were all about getting my bearings. And being around people from hostel to hostel was a great way to keep my mind off missing my other life too much or pining for Warren too often. I bought a calling card and tried him repeatedly when there was a payphone available. But the time difference and our own personal schedules made those connections few and far between. He was on my mind constantly, it seemed, and my heart longed for him acutely. I knew we would be having so much more fun together.

But, alas, we were not together, and I was in Australia! New places, new people…. An onslaught to the senses, really. And for the most part, I was loving it. Picking clams on the beach and cooking them over bonfires with fellow travelers from all over the world.

These new people I was proud to call friends. Hiking mountains – that admittedly kicked my ass – to watch the sunrise from what felt like the top of the world. Drinking way too much and having way too much fun. It was surreal, this reality that was suddenly mine.
And I was enjoying the hell out of it.

***

Within a surprisingly short amount of time, my life had turned into one big party after another, with diverse and offbeat individuals flowing through my days like fish with the tides. Bonfires on the beach after a day of swimming in the waves. Getting drunk with friends newly met and passing out in the sand. Waking up on someone's floor, still in my bathing suit. Trying to find my way back to the hostel in the dark after a few beers and not even knowing what town I was in. I was surrounded by people my age doing the same thing, so it didn't seem precarious or risky at all. Crazy, stupid stuff, really. But quite fun!

It was easy to get a false sense of security when always surrounded by others. Almost like I wasn't actually traveling alone at all, but continually had someone watching my back. But, as most travelers eventually come to realize, there was nothing further from the truth.

I had the great fortune to have a home-base in Sydney with friends of friends who had an apartment there. Jim and Cate were a few years older than I, and they lived part-time in Sydney and part-time in Glenwood Springs, Colorado, where I lived before my Australian adventure and where my sister and her hubby lived. Cate was from the States and Jim was Australian, and this is how they decided to live after they got married. For good reason, Jim didn't want to give up his residency in Australia, and in order for him to keep in good standing with his homeland country, he had to prove that he was in Australia at least every six months. Luckily for me, they were happy to lend me a hand by giving me an address for mail to be sent and a place to crash if and when I was in the big city.

This arrangement was a Godsend because it made it possible for me to receive mail, which, in those days, with no cell phones, social media, or texting, was a huge deal. I was beyond thankful. Also, it was great to have people from home to chat with when they were around. Giving me a connection to my people every once in a while, no matter how removed, was invaluable. They would regale me with skiing and snowboarding stories and update me on the shenanigans of friends and mutual acquaintances from our little Colorado town. I would drink in the welcomed familiarity and let it fill my soul. In the six months that I spent in Australia, I took advantage of their hospitality more than a few times with utter gratitude, while trying not to become that annoying guest!

But when I was traveling, I was alone. And it was best to remember that the people I met along the way were not friends, but fun connections. Case in point: one night a group of us from the hostel-of-the-week went out for drinks. Of course, as was usual, a few drinks turned into many. I remember the night vividly and keep it in my memory as a reminder. The place was packed, all with fellow travelers like me. Our group had our own large wooden picnic table on an outdoor stone patio. There were at least thirty more tables, all occupied by more young, drunk travelers. Everyone was in some degree of substance or alcohol-fueled euphoria.

A young woman at the far end of the patio jumped on her table and started dancing to the loud music. All fun and games until she lost her footing and fell. The patio floor was made of bricks. She landed on her head. Within an instant, everything went silent. A few people at her table, and I mean very few, jumped to her side to see if she was alive, and assess whether she was ok, though none of them were in the medical field. But, more shockingly, most of her group hastily took off. They left.

Scattered into oblivion without a backwards glance. There was a hint of blood involved, but nothing overly gory. An ambulance eventually came and took her to get the care she needed.

The party came to an abrupt halt. What I most remember about that vivid evening is that the people who were supposed to be her friends left her without even knowing her condition, before she received any medical aid, without even trying to secure help for her. Someone at another table ran to the owners to have them call for help. Her buddies just left. It was a hugely unfortunate event for that girl, but an enormous learning experience for many others of us there that night. When you are traveling solo, you are always solo, no matter how many other people may be around. NEVER take for granted that someone will be there – or stay – to help you should trouble strike.

Now maybe this is my personal baggage talking – maybe abandonment issues, maybe low self-worth, maybe trusting others isn't my strong suit (understatement of the century). But the fundamental reality that I am and was alone was a harsh and necessary lesson. If traveler was the path I chose, I needed to understand the potential, yet very real, consequences I could face. Especially when alcohol, and usually some drugs, were involved.

How easy to feel a false sense of security among the seemingly instant intimacy of new friends. I had to be careful and not take stupid and unnecessary chances. The Universe gave me the lesson I needed to take to heart, unfortunately at that girl's expense. To her, I channeled healing energy and prayers for a swift and thorough recovery. Now it was up to me to take heed. The opportunities were ample.

This great land of Oz is well known for the astonishing array of critters that call it home. From the exotic, cute, cuddly types to the deadly, venomous kind, there is no shortage of shock value in the world of Australia's animal kingdom. In fact, the smallest of the earth's continents has the third highest percentage of deadly creatures. I know people who have vowed to never step foot on this continent due to its sixty-six venomous species.

Of course, I knew nothing of this before starting my travels. And, honestly, there were few instances of face-to-face introductions to the venomous threats. Not none, but few, fortunately. However, there was one shocking introduction to a species of flying mammal (not even venomous) that I will not easily forget.

A fellow traveler from Holland, Belia, and I had decided to take a stroll into town to see a movie. Murwillumbah was a relatively small town of almost 10,000 people, located in
New South Wales just on the edge of Queensland. It was a safe and friendly place, and the movie theatre was only about a mile and a half from the hostel. Belia and I enjoyed our early evening stroll into town in the dwindling daylight.

By the time our movie let out, the sun had completely set. It was overcast, no starlight to guide us. Neither of us had brought a flashlight. So, we headed home under the dark night sky. As we reached the turnoff to the hostel, just under one of the few streetlights we had encountered, we heard a loud rustling from the tree we were passing. We could not believe our eyes as what felt like a horror scene began to unfold. The tree seemingly came to life. From the rustling emerged an enormous bat-like creature that took flight right over our heads. Its wings casting us again into darkness.

We were both terrified, certain Dracula would soon sink his teeth into our pulsating jugulars. Ducking our heads, screaming, and running as fast as our feet would carry us, we made it back to the hostel unscathed but mentally tortured. Our fear consumed us! We were nearly crying with anxiety. When we told our chilling tale to fellow hostelers, a few of whom were better acquainted with Australian wildlife, we all got a good laugh. Our flying devil was not, in fact, Dracula, but a fruit bat. Otherwise known as a flying fox. The largest bat in the world. We were validated in our assessment of its huge size!

Fruit bats have a wingspan of up to five feet, with a head-to-toe measurement of about sixteen inches. Having no knowledge that such a thing existed, both of us were mortified when it was seemingly flying for our throats! After getting more acquainted with them, it turns out that these bats are actually super cute. They only eat fruit, hence the name, and their huge, glossy eyes, little bat ears, and doglike snouts, make them look like innocent cartoon characters. They really are quite adorable. Belia and I took comfort in knowing that there was no way we were in danger of eternal life via bloodsucking. But it sure was one hell of an introduction to the world's largest bat!

***

Australia is home to the largest coral reef in the world. In. The. World. It runs along the coastline of the northeast part of the country and is approximately 1,500 miles long. That's just the length! One thousand five hundred miles. That's the distance from Miami to Massachusetts. To say the very least, it's fucking huge. And I was there. Right in the middle of it all, about to embark on a three-day sailing trip through the Whitsunday Islands out of Airlie Beach.

I actually felt bittersweet about the sailing trip. Although I was excited and it sounded fantastic, I was taking the sailing cruise because I'd just learned that my ears wouldn't stabilize pressure well enough for me to get my diving certificate. As with most visitors to the Great Barrier Reef, I came here to scuba dive so that I could explore real-time and up-close, the world's largest underwater masterpiece.

But the Universe had other plans. After enrolling in diving classes, it was mandatory to have a doctor's exam to receive my certificate. Just a short visit to the doctor revealed the highly inconvenient fact that one of my eardrums was pierced; I could not equalize pressure underwater. No diving certificate for me. And how, exactly, did I come to have a pierced eardrum?

Hmmm. Well, it turns out that just before I left for this big solo adventure to the great land of Oz, some friends took me out for a celebratory sushi dinner. My friend, Jen, got herself all nice and lit and then thought it would be funny to stick her chopstick in my ear.

The next morning, I woke to a bit of blood on my pillow. But, of course, I quickly wrote it off as nothing because there was no way in hell I was going to the doctor. First, I had no time to make an appointment before leaving. And second, more importantly, I had no insurance and would not waste money from my travel fund for such a triviality. I had absolutely no clue that something like that could and would come back to haunt me in such a way! Well, shit, thanks a lot, Jen.

The boat was a fifty-foot sailboat. In addition to the captain and cook, there were twelve passengers for the three-day excursion. We were all within five years of age of one another, so we were a young, enthusiastic, energetic group. It didn't take long to discover that our collective chemistry was extraordinary.

Within an hour of setting sail, half of us lined up on deck next to each other and mooned passing boats! We joked and laughed until we cried. We rejoiced in each other's company. It was an incredible experience to know that we all "clicked." After a few excursions with people who didn't get along so well for days on end, this was a welcome relief. I was the only American in our group. The others were from Israel, Germany, Sweden, and the UK.

The first night aboard, Gary – one of the Brits – and I sat on the bow and just bathed in the absolute beauty of the boat at anchor in a pristine, isolated harbor. The temps were absolutely perfect for a tank top and sarong, the seas were calm and inviting, and the skies were cloudless and full of stars.

Thoughts of Warren had been consuming me and Gary was the perfect escape I needed. After dinner was served, rain clouds stealthily crept over us for most of the night. We all disappeared below deck and played games and acquainted ourselves better until we happily passed out. Gary and I became particularly well-acquainted.

The next morning, the skies cleared up, but the seas did not. The continual pitching of the boat made me nauseous. I found that the only reprive I had from motion sickness was to be in the water. So, I spent most of the day with my snorkel equipment on, in the ocean, basking in the splendor of the Great Barrier Reef. I wasn't the only one who wasn't faring well because of the seas. The poor Englishman was hurling overboard.

He was mortified, and the detritus was disgusting, but one perk of his distress was that the reef fish swarmed the boat in a mass-feeding frenzy! Gross, yes, but sometimes you simply have to make the best of a shitty situation. In between bouts of vomiting, he was blessed with an abundance of beautiful sea creatures! As for me, I floated well away from the food source and silently enjoyed the surfeit of fish it attracted. Dear bloke, so sorry for your misery. But, thanks! As we say in the States, "You took one for the team. Good job!"

Lisa Ruoff

Oh. My. God. I can't begin to describe the astounding and miraculous world beneath the ocean's surface. But I will do my best to give it the credit it deserves. The vivid sights and sounds of the underwater city visible through my "sea glasses" threatened sensory overload. Mysterious and mesmerizing noises of crunching and clicking will remain an enigma to me until my dying day.

The plethora of schools of fish, by the thousands, with shimmering and brilliant colors, was almost beyond the comprehension of this mere mortal. Big fish, little fish, lone fish, schools of hundreds of fish, eels, manta rays, sea turtles, moving coral, hard coral, orange and purple coral, white sand, rocky ridges, steep ledges over seemingly endless abysses. And all of it so rich and vibrant! Did I do it justice?
Hardly. How thankful and humbled I am to have experienced this miracle of nature personally.

At the time, there was no way for me to comprehend how utterly privileged I was to have the experience of seeing the Great Barrier Reef in its full glory, as a healthy ecosystem. In stark contrast, I visited the reefs of the Mayan Riviera decades later, in 2022. My experience was devastating.

The reefs off Mexico's East Coast were, at one time, just as diverse, beautiful, and alive as those off the coast of Australia. Albeit not as large, but just as healthy. My visit in 2022 was like a two-by-four across my temple. It hit hard. Rising ocean temperatures had caused coral bleaching, especially in recent years. The once stunning reefs were more than 80% dead. Heavy, dark green algae swayed in the currents while clinging to the coral beds they had overtaken. There were fish, but very few compared to what I had seen in previous years. And the tourism that continued to exceed capacity just kept growing.

I was very confused at first, thinking that perhaps my eyes were deceiving me. Maybe the coral was doing okay. But then I realized that most of the tourists had never seen a living coral reef and therefore had no idea that they were witnessing the death of an entire ecosystem. The local economy was treating it all like the emperor's new clothes. It wasn't only business as usual; business was booming. People kept coming and paying higher prices to look at dead reefs. It was beyond heartbreaking; it was absolute insanity. It took two days to acclimate my grief and disbelief about the situation to stop my tears from flowing.

On the beautiful shoreline, I sat and prayed to the Ocean for forgiveness. And then I performed reiki to try to return whatever small amount of life energy possible to the reef system. It was the best I could do. And I know it wasn't enough. To watch the planet deteriorate before my eyes, in less than the span of one lifetime, was (and is) devastating enough to drown myself in tequila.

But maybe that's the point of travel. To experience both the light and the dark. Experience does not inherently have a positive context. In the wise voice of Madeleine L'Engle, "Maybe you have to know the darkness before you appreciate the light." In my utter astonishment at the horrid state of the ocean's reef systems, I simultaneously appreciated my previous reef experiences exponentially more. Gratitude and grief. Light and dark. Sorrow and appreciation.

Our three-day sailing itinerary included a stop at an island that was home to a cave with ancient Aboriginal petroglyphs. My first exposure to Aboriginal heritage was while hiking Mt. Warning, named thus by Captain Cook in 1770 when he had to change course due to the dangerous offshore reefs that lay beneath the shadow of the mountain's peak.

It's the highest peak in the region and the most easterly, making it the first bit of land to see sunrise. It's a magical place. Hence the Aboriginal name, Wollumbin, which means, among other interpretations, Cloud Catcher. Wollumbin and the land surrounding it are sacred to the Bundjalung people, who were the original custodians of the land tens of thousands of years ago.

Now, I was visiting the ancient sites of the Ngaro peoples who made their lives on the shores of this abundant reef. Wow! What a place to call home – that's all I kept thinking. Unbelievable beauty and splendor with all the abundance of the world's largest reef system right there at your front door. Their way of life fascinated me, water sign that I am. As I surveyed the petroglyphs of what appeared to be sea turtles, I could feel the power of the ocean beneath me as I paddled my ironbark canoe among the stunning reefs, teeming with life, providing a smorgasbord for my family's dinner.

But their seafaring society was destroyed by traders, colonists, and the Australian Native Police. It is said the Native Police Corps in 1870 forcibly relocated the Ngaro to a penal colony on Palm Island or to Brampton Island's lumber mills. A tragic end to a vibrant culture, I sense a theme emerging. Gratitude and grief. Light and dark. Sorrow and appreciation. I felt honored to get a glimpse of the Ngaro and their world.

And thankful to receive a bit of its bounty. Just as seafood was the primary staple of the Ngaro diet, it was the core source of sustenance for our sailing excursion. The riches of the sea and the chef's prowess did not disappoint.

Food was and is – a huge part of the traveling life. It seems to be either feast or famine, and very little balance in between. For example, for three days we gorged ourselves on delicious and abundant seafood of all sorts. Then – for the hostelers – the return to the "real" world of travel life means living on ramen noodles and peanut butter sandwiches made in shared hostel kitchens. The first hostel joke you may hear about food goes something like this: A traveler enters a fine dining establishment and says to the hostess: "Table for one, please. Food for three."

I quickly found a very important bit of information while traveling, especially in Australia. I was a seafood eating vegetarian, properly known as a pescatarian, but I don't believe that word existed back in 1995 (at least, I hadn't heard of it). As a traveler who didn't eat meat, my gastronomic life was extremely challenging and rendered my palate very unsatisfied much of the time.

In Australia, they consider a parsley garnish on top of a slab of beef to be a salad! Honestly, most of the times I told food establishments I was vegetarian, the answer was usually "No worries, there are onions and peas in that meat pie." Not exactly what I was thinking…But the mouthwatering delicacies that were bestowed upon us during that sailing excursion were divine. I appreciated them beyond any measure and savored every delectable bite.

Over those three days at sea, not only did all of us have a magical time sharing our reef experience, but I believe we were all pleasantly surprised by our genuine connection as friends. Instead of hastily moving on to the next great adventure when the sail ended, we all met for one last night of revelry. One more night of unforgettable food, unlimited drink, and the twelve of us grinding and mashing on the dancefloor in yet more drunken revelry.

Gary and I ended the evening disappearing to our shared room before he boarded a bus the next morning. Our brief fling seemed to relieve my heartache over Warren for a few days, and admittedly, those few days were a wonderful distraction, both physically and emotionally. The entirety of the sail was exactly the boost my soul needed. By the end of that weekend, I came to believe the pierced eardrum was a blessing in disguise, the Universe at work in ways big and small (but I still held a grudge against Jen for that whole chopstick debacle).

* * *

> "Good girls go to heaven. Bad girls go everywhere."
> –Mae West

After a few months apart, both Warren and I decided that we needed to be together and would meet again in South Africa after my Australia adventure was over. We were miserable without each other. I spent countless nights silently crying myself to sleep in hostel after hostel, out of sheer longing for him. The sporadic payphone calls just simply weren't enough to sustain my sense of connectedness to him. The "we" I knew and loved felt – and was – so very far away. The time difference didn't help. Despite our sporadic communication, he was forever on my mind. It was excruciating to be apart.

And, according to him, our separation was wreaking havoc on him, too. Even though the next few months would be a tremendous challenge for both of us, I could deal with just about anything knowing that I was going to be with my love again, relatively soon! I already had a return ticket to the States at the end of my six months down under. Now, my focus was to make enough money for airfare from Colorado to South Africa. Thus inspired, my search for employment began.

First, there was what I call the Motorbike Outback Escapade. I had made a good friend in Vikki, a fellow backpacker and "Kiwi" (meaning from New Zealand where the kiwi is the national bird). We were fortunate to be offered an opportunity to round up sheep by motorcycle for the sheering season. The farm was in a place outside of Mungundi, a border town on the edge of what is known as the Australian Outback.

The Outback comprises about 75% of the Australian continent but is home to only about 5% of its population. Basically, it is the big, empty, dry land of the interior of Australia, although some of it encompasses the monsoonal north country as well. It's remote. Very remote. And is known for its desolate landscape and harsh conditions. And I was about to go chase sheep around on a motorbike out there! Woo-hoo!!

Vikki and I were bursting with excitement and anticipation for this most unusual employment opportunity. Each of us had nearly exhausted our funds. We needed jobs. This gig was not guaranteed. From what we understood, if all went well after a week, the farmer would reimburse us for our transportation to the farm and would pay us hourly. Room and board were also included in the deal. It certainly didn't sound like a five-star hotel, but it was better than camping. We were prepared. And, as it happened, we would be there for my birthday. Who gets to say they were herding sheep by motorcycle in the Australian Outback for their 24th birthday? I mean, really.

To get to the farm, we had to hitch a ride with the local mail truck from Mungundi, which only ventured that distance once a week. Naturally, it was going to cost us and, indeed, it wasn't cheap. We were told the trip would take about four hours, and we had to sit in the back with all the packages. Our backpacks would make sufficiently comfortable seating, we were sure.

Of course, the night before our departure, we ended up carousing with the bartenders at the local pub until the wee hours of the morning. Consequently, that four-hour truck ride wasn't the least bit comfortable at all. In fact, it was quite miserable. Dealing with self-inflicted discomfort was becoming quite normal given our propensity to party, or "getting pissed" as they say in the vernacular. Hungover, but undaunted, we arrived intrepid and intact, ready to round up sheep. And both of us overcame the need to toss our marbles despite the torturous lurching of the truck over copious ruts in the road.

The farm was run by a couple who had three young children, a bunch of cows, and a few hundred sheep. Gordon, the man of the farm, met us at the road when the mail truck dropped us off, and showed us to our sleeping quarters. The shearers' quarters (where the people shearing the sheep stay) were already spoken for by the actual shearers, who had not arrived yet but were expected within the next day or two. We had the privilege of taking what I referred to as the next step down. Let's just say the cabin he showed us made me miss my tent!

Disgusting would have been giving it way too much praise. But we weren't deterred (yet). Both Vikki and I were still determined that this was a wonderful opportunity and that we just had to go with the flow (which is actually an Aussie phrase. Who knew?!). We certainly didn't want a reputation as the whiny little princesses.

So, we settled into our new accommodations for the evening. Trudging past the kitchen and into the bedroom, with two single beds, I tried to overlook the dirt, dust, and grime that had accumulated sometime between the last inhabitants and us. Those layers of filth were thick. Now, keep in mind that we were backpackers, not tourists! We were used to sub-par standards. But that place really defied all levels of sanitation and comfort.

It looked like it was salvaged from a deserted trailer park, but it wasn't even a trailer. The chipped and peeling vinyl tiles on the kitchen floor were an upgrade from the raw planks in the bedroom and bathroom. It was too dark to notice at that point, but we could actually see through the slits in the planks to the dirt ground below.

The cockroaches in the bed should have been a clue. There were sheets on the beds, but both of us chose to pull out our sleeping bags instead of risking it. After kicking the cockroaches out, we ventured into the bathroom.

Pulling back the shower curtain was an invitation to the family of frogs in the bathtub to start serenading us with their chorus of croaking. Unfortunately for them, their quest for some kind of moisture had come up empty. I didn't have the heart to put them outside in the dry dirt and left them there to wait for me to test the plumbing. The thankful frogs happily regaled us with their symphony throughout the night. How hospitable of them. Would we have to pay extra for this enthusiastic welcome?

Then it was into the kitchen to conjure up some kind of meal from our packs, since it didn't appear Gordon was going to serve us fine cuisine anytime soon. He'd left some milk and cheese for us. Remarkably, the fridge looked a bit cleaner than the rest of the place. After finding a somewhat passably clean rag and wiping down the table, we sat in rickety chairs and started in on our hodgepodge of a dinner.

Within a few minutes, a terrifying shriek had us jumping out of our seats in fright. There was a screaming cat stuck to the middle of the kitchen screen door, all claws, teeth, and fur in an utter fury. Seems that the cabin was also home to an abundance of feral cats that didn't especially like people.

Jesus fucking Christ!

But that wasn't all. One last little present before we tried to get some shut-eye. And this was my absolute favorite: two huge, hairy spiders on the wall in the bedroom. Ask anyone who knows anything about me, and they will tell you I absolutely loathe and fear these members of the arachnid family.

Everything until that moment was manageable, but spiders! Oh, shit… Thank God for Vikki that night. She took control and rid our boudoir of the gigantic Wolf spiders, thereby saving my ass and my sanity. Did you know those mother fuckers jump? They JUMP! Huge, hairy, jumping spiders?!!!! WTF?

The next morning, Gordon woke us at 6:30 am. Since the shearers hadn't arrived yet, there was no need for us to round up the sheep. So, we were pressed into service to mix and pour concrete from sunrise until sunset. Let me fill you in on some things I learned about the Outback that day.

It's hot. I mean, beyond-comprehension-kind-of-hot. Eyeball sweating, hellfire hot. Not-enough-water-in-the-world-to-cool-and-rehydrate-hot. But there's no water anywhere out there, so that's not an issue. And there are no trees. Not one. No shade anywhere. The bugs are relentless. They are the spawn of Satan sent straight from the bowels of the Underworld; I swear it. The snakes can and will kill you if you don't kill them first. They're colossal and swift. Lastly, working concrete without gloves tends to eat the skin right off your hands.

Here's the scene: we are clueless, out of shape, single, female backpackers looking to get an Outback experience, mixing and pouring concrete for fence posts with no gloves, in the searing heat, with no shade, continually swarmed by biting insects, all while trying to keep a lookout for ten-footlong killer snakes, for approximately, oh, I'd say, about twenty-million hours straight! How the hell did I get myself into these situations?!

Besides eating the skin off of our hands, the backbreaking work of mixing and pouring concrete also kicked our out-of-shape asses. We learned why Australian farmers wear those funny hats with things hanging from the brim – they mimic a horsetail, swishing all the bugs away as you move your head. They're called cork hats because they were originally made by hanging corks off the rim of the hat. Brilliant, really. Our sunburned flesh taught us to wear long sleeve shirts, even in temps hot enough to fry an egg.

And yes, we finally got our opportunity to kill a snake. An eastern brown snake, highly venomous and about six-feet long (which looks about twenty-feet long when you are trying to kill it with a shovel). By saying that "we got our opportunity" to kill it, I mean, Vikki and I both refused to get out of the truck and appointed Gordon executioner. I didn't necessarily have an aversion to snakes (unlike my mother, who would have had a heart attack), but then again, normal snakes in my world weren't six-feet long and capable of taking my life. Sorry, but I had my limits.

And about that absolutely off-the-wall adventure we were to have had that made us the envy of other travelers who took more conventional paths to replenish their bank accounts . . . Well, we never did get to herd sheep on motorcycles. The damned shearers never showed up.

Our Motorbike Outback Escapade had become a farce. We soon realized that Gordon never had any intention of paying a freakin' cent for one minute of our work. Yes, the room and board were free – how fucking generous of him! We especially enjoyed the complimentary screeching feral cats clinging to the screen door nightly. Knowing that the mail truck was our only way out of there, and that it arrived just once a week, we were marooned in the desert and had to make the best of it. It wasn't fun. but we lived through it. It wasn't the birthday celebration I'd envisioned, but I was gifted with lots of stories to share. And let's just say, visiting the Australian Outback is now off my bucket list.

***

"We don't believe in ghosts, Mrs. Phipps."
"Don't matter if you believe in them or not. If they're there, they're there."
- Joan Lowery Nixon, The Haunting

I was on closing duty, which meant I had to go upstairs to the event room, turn out the lights in the window, and make sure everything was put away before closing the restaurant for the night. This one singular job filled me with foreboding, but everyone who had the closing shift had to do it. And that night was my turn.

I hesitantly headed up the stairs, dreading the next few minutes, as we all did at that point in the shift. Opening the door ever so slowly and taking stock of the room with a vast sweep of my eye, my movements turned from slow and trepidatious to speedy and alert. Get in and out as quickly as possible. The normal routine: start at the left and move briskly, clockwise, around the table.

Put the plates away on the sideboard, circumnavigate the big serving table in the middle of the room to the window on the other side, and unplug the plastic candle lights shining in the window. Dash to the next window and repeat. And then, as if on cue, as it did every night, regardless of who was on duty, the room turned freezing cold, and the door slammed shut. Luckily, it never locked itself, but whatever was in there with me made its point loud and clear: GET OUT! Being a Scorpio, with a birthday two days from Halloween, I've been known to tap into other realms now and then and have actually tried to reach out to "the other side" once or twice. Sometimes spirits are just souls that have gotten stuck and are looking for a bit of assistance to move on. Other times, I've found certain spirits or energies have a purpose such as facilitating resolution of a specific problem. A little helping hand from the other side, so to speak. And yet other run-ins have proven that some spirits are just there. Not menacing or necessarily helpful, but just kind of like us living beings, they're just doing their thing.

But not with the energies at the Inn. It happened the same way every night, freaking me out just as much every time. The temperature in that room could drop willy-nilly during the course of the day, but we all knew it would happen after dark when one of us was up there alone. As far as I know, nobody knew the story behind the ghost living in the event room. But it certainly exuded very threatening, negative energy!

And it surely wasn't the only spirit in the house. Fortunately, we didn't offer overnight lodging anymore, as they used the upstairs rooms for private parties instead of accommodations. But the place was built in the mid-1800's and had its fair share of stories, as well as secrets. There were always weird things happening at the Inn. Lights turned off and on for no reason, faucets started flowing water or stopped with no twist of the knobs, things fell from shelves and crashed to the floor. And their favorite trick: immediate and inexplicable plummeting temperatures. Crazy fast. Crazy cold. Crazy freaky.

The shower for the female employees was on the side of the building. After taking my shower one day, I pulled aside the curtain, and there, in the foggy condensation of the bathroom mirror, was the handwritten scribble "Boo!!" I had most definitely locked the door; there was no way anyone could have entered to play a prank on me.

As thick as potato soup, the energy in the room was full of tension. Totally eerie, that place was!

Still, it was a real paying job. I can't say it was the best job I ever had, and it certainly didn't pay extremely well, but it was a million steps above the Outback fiasco! Even with the nasty, negative spirit realm often in pursuit of me…

The place was called the White Horse Inn in Berrima, an historic village in the southern highlands of New South Wales. I had been interviewed by the owner, an older woman of obvious prosperous means, who resided in Sydney. A couple in their early thirties, who lived on the premises, managed the Inn for her. Fortunately for me, she was able to keep one person on staff "off the record," meaning she would overlook my lack of work visa and pay me cash.

My job was to be a server at the Inn, which, I was told, had a thriving clientele of tourists enjoying the rural hillsides of the drive between Sydney and Australia's capital of Canberra. My funds were quickly dwindling. I really didn't care what the position was as long as it paid and was bearable. I had to shell out an enormous sum for the mail truck to and from that Outback sheep farm. I'd just enough money to get the train out to the Inn, with a few bucks to spare for a celebratory drink at the local pub with my new workmates.

There were around seven to ten employees on staff at the Inn at any given time. Women's quarters were behind the Inn, in what we called the Carriage House. There was no water in the Carriage House, and we had to use the shower and bathroom on the side entrance of the Inn (the one with the good-humored ghost). We all slept in one big room that had single beds in a line. If we all liked each other, it was like a sleepover with best friends. If we didn't, well, it wasn't such a great setup. I lived with a few of both during those months.

The male employees had their own house about a mile down the road, in town. Needless to say, their house was the party house. The guys had their own bedrooms, so even if they didn't want to party, they got to close their doors. Lucky bastards!

My months in Berrima were a mixed bag. The work part was your standard service industry fare – little money, lots of labor, lousy management, shitty conditions. And, of course, the uniforms took a bit of getting used to. In an effort to recreate the atmosphere of the Inn, to bring an air of authenticity to the dining experience, we wore peasant dresses – big, black, bulky skirts down to our ankles with long sleeve, button up, white blouses tucked into our waistbands.

Those of us with long tresses had to put our hair up. And to finish the look: little white bonnets. Not exactly the most fashionable or appealing of outfits. But we did look like serving wenches from the 1800's so I give them a passing grade for costuming. The food was good and free for the employees, which was a huge plus. The party house was a welcome place to hang out. I appreciated being with people I would consider friends. And for the most part, tips were decent.

The couple that managed the place also lived on the premises, in an apartment behind the Inn. Gisella was the woman's name, and she immediately took a dislike to me. I don't know her exact reasons, but she made it very clear, not only to me but to the rest of the staff, that she didn't like Americans.

Whenever she could, she made my life as miserable as possible. She would make me work late (with no overtime compensation), assign me the terrible shifts, or ensure my cleaning chores were the worst of the list. Oh, what a joy of a woman to work for! But, really, as far as restaurant work went, those conditions were comparable to the norm, and not unbearable. As long as I just went with the flow.

Solitude wasn't the only thing that was difficult in Berrima. It was a tiny town, and there wasn't a hell of a lot to do besides patronize the local pub to drink and shoot pool. I spent most of my free time either missing Warren immensely or trying not to think about him. Drink. Smoke. Miss Warren. Repeat. It made for two very long months. But that time enabled me to refill my coffers and continue my adventure.

***

My employment at the White Horse Inn ended between Christmas and New Years Eve of 1995. One of my most memorable experiences was celebrating New Year's Eve down by the Sydney Harbor with two very close friends and co-workers from the Inn, Marie and Siobhan, from Ireland. Fireworks, champagne, millions (literally) of happy, partying people in the crowd, all against the backdrop of the beautifully lit Sydney Opera House shimmering in the reflection of the ocean harbor.

Incredible! After two months of living in a desolate little village, my senses were overwhelmed and alive with excitement! The sights, smells, sounds…All of it just made me giddy. At one point, we had an extra bottle of champagne and didn't want to chug it before we caught a train to our next destination, so I jumped into a group of punks – all chained leather and blue mohawks – and gave it to them.

Immediately, I became a Goddess.

Lisa Ruoff

It was New Year's Eve, everyone was full of love and light, and I was so very happy! To top off a most memorable evening, my New Years' present was a long-awaited phone conversation with Warren. Ah, such bliss to connect again, even for a short time, and over a phone line of a few thousand miles. Merely hearing his voice was enough to transform me into a giggly, love-struck teenager for the rest of the night. What a glorious way to ring in the New Year!

Shortly before my status changed to gainfully employed, I caught a ride with a guy going from Darwin on the North Coast down to Sydney. My plan was to fly to New Zealand and explore there for a bit. Unfortunately for both of us, on the way down the coast, we hit a routine police block on the highway. They were looking for drugs, of which we had none. Thank God. I'm not quite sure how that happened but was over-the-top grateful to whatever guardian angels took care of that potentially disastrous detail. Illicit substance possession overseas? Didn't need that.

Bite of the Travel Bug

They nailed us for lack of insurance and registration. Since I was driving at the time, I was ticketed for driving his car without proper coverage (which I thought was absolutely unfair since it wasn't my car nor my responsibility). He was ticketed for not having updated registration or proper insurance. The police didn't accept my case, though, and it cost us both a small fortune! Yeah, and that's really focusing on "protecting and serving," right? Fucking cops…

The worst part was I was counting on that money for my flight to New Zealand. The exorbitant traffic fine put the nix on that. The whole situation really pissed me off, but I promised myself, before the end of my Australian adventure, I would take a much less expensive side trip to Tasmania instead. Why not? Smaller island, closer in proximity, cheaper plane ticket. I didn't know a damned thing about Tasmania, but I would soon.

***

"And into the forest I go, to lose my mind and find my soul."
–John Muir

Only a few days into the New Year, I jumped on a short flight to the small island of Tasmania, just south of the tip of Eastern Australia. The only clue I had about this island before I arrived was that it was wild. As in, untouched woods-and-forest kind of wild, not party wild! And I was super eager to get back in touch with nature for a while. I'd been carrying all of my camping gear around Australia, and it was actually going to see some action. Yay! My soul was always most fulfilled when I was in the woods (still is) and I was absolutely crawling out of my skin with excitement to be "roughing it" again.

As usual, I spent the first few nights in hostels to get my bearings and make a plan. Tas – as I took to calling it – was a different blueprint from the mainland, though. Very limited public transportation made it quite challenging to get to and from remote areas. And remote areas were where I wanted to be. So, it was time to change how I went about doing things.

Most of our lives, growing up in America, we were taught fear. It was done out of love and for our best good, of course. I understand that. But the decision to start hitchhiking, as a solo female, in remote areas of an island known solely for its cartoon character of a devil, is a great place to undo a lifetime of teachings. What the hell, right? If you're gonna go, go big. I hit the road with my thumb out, hoping that the person who chose to stop and pick me up wouldn't be a serial killer or rapist.

There I was, standing on the side of the highway on the outskirts of Devonport, Tasmania, with my thumb out, begging for a free ride to the middle of nowhere. Devonport was one of the biggest cities in Tasmania, population approximately 20,000 residents. Not exactly big by American standards. Everything I owned was at my feet.

And so, it was…

It took about twenty minutes until I found myself scrambling into the back of an ASPCA dog rescue truck, making friends with a cute, happy, little, yippy dog named Murphy, and Murphy's seemingly harmless homosapien dad. Being a driver for the ASPCA offered little opportunity for human contact, I guess.

The joyful driver was delighted to accommodate a first timer to his beautiful island. He took me on a three-hour tour of the Tasmanian coastline, followed by the nearby mountainous region where I longed to lose myself. He dropped me about two kilometers from a remote campground in Cradle Mountain National Park. Absolutely perfect. Thank you, Universe, once again, for having my back!

That evening, I pitched my tent on the outskirts of the campground, not wanting to be near anyone. I had no need to worry, as it seemed there wasn't a single soul for miles, at least. Not human, anyway. The sun was starting its descent as I organized my gear for the night. I quickly found that I had an uninvited guest following me around making quite the noisy racket. A baby Tasmanian devil somehow had decided that I would have to suffice in lieu of its lost mother. It was utterly adorable – besides that terrible screeching sound it was making. For a brief while, I felt quite privileged by the little guy's presence and relished my role as a new mother.

    Still, Tasmanian devils, I'd heard, were named because of their temperament. I didn't get intimately acquainted with the little beasts, but according to National Geographic, they tend to fly into a rage when threatened by a predator, fighting for a mate, or defending a meal. Early European settlers dubbed them "devils" after witnessing displays of teeth-baring, lunging, spinning, and an array of spinechilling guttural growls. Hence, the cartoon character that follows after its namesake.

    Not a good thing, to have a baby devil latching onto me in a deserted campground before going to sleep in my paper-thin tent. I mean, really, Universe, very subtle. A freaking DEVIL!! Reluctantly, I set out to walk around the campground perimeters hoping the cute little thing would wander off toward its home, wherever that might be. It took some time, and it was dark when my plan finally succeeded, but indeed, the baby devil took his leave, off to find his rightful mother.

I was privy to the screeching of the adults that night, not too far away from my camping oasis. I hoped that meant joy over the return of the young one. And I tell you the Europeans were right; Tasmanian devils make horrific sounds! Worse than a kid learning violin. Worse than a baby shrieking or nails on a chalkboard. More unearthly than any noise I have ever heard an animal make. Yes, "devil" seemed an apt name.

Despite the blood-curdling screams, I knew the devils were really no threat to me and I found it to be an absolutely thrilling experience, lying in my tent in a remote Tasmanian park, listening to the sounds of the boisterous Tasmanian devils. How many people on the planet can say they fell asleep, isolated in their tent, to the sounds of the Tasmanian devils fighting? Mating? I was really upping my own game. Taking another step out of the comfort zone. There are instances in life that just light up my soul – this was one of them and I was full of gratitude!

As for the wildlife of Tas, my hopes were being fulfilled. Sightings were far more frequent than on the mainland, simply because I was living in the woods. I was ecstatic. On the mainland, there were kangaroos. I didn't see many, but a few. And, despite being the country's mascot, roos were not well-liked, given the damage they inflicted on crops and other habitats. Here on Tas, there were more wallabies than kangaroos from what I saw.

A wallaby is a mini version of a kangaroo, with a much nicer disposition. Kangaroos, although a welcomed exotic sight to my American eyes, are not only nasty beasts, but they have some pretty powerful muscles to back their bravado. Basically, you don't fuck with kangaroos because they are highly capable of killing a human with little effort. But these little wally hoppers would come right up and eat out of my hand. Not a threatening bone in their bodies.

And there were wombats. Oh my God, wombats were my favorite! They were like big, monotone guinea pigs on crack. Standing just below knee height, and covered in brownish-gray fur, they were friendly but timid creatures. If I was patient enough, I could coax one to come to me at the campsite, but it took an hour or so of just sitting in my chair, absolutely dead still.

Then this large, oddly adorable animal would shyly approach to take a much-appreciated morsel of food out of my hand. They were built like cement bricks. They were rock solid! It was a commonly known fact that if you hit a wallaby with your car, the wallaby would be fine, but your tire would be flat (maybe a bit morbid, but truthful). In the remote reaches of Tasmania, a flat tire you do not want. Actually, the same was said about cane toads on the mainland of Oz. Those huge amphibians were bountiful in and around the cane fields and were extremely detrimental to unsuspecting automobiles.

To say that Tasmania was incredible would be an injustice. Natural beauty and solitude enveloped me, the elements my body and soul craved. Not even the rains that were to render me "housebound" in my tent could dampen my appreciation for these gifts.

Such beauty abounds in Tas. Crater Mountain National Park was just one of many national parks on the island – over half of the country is protected public lands – and that's where I spent the better part of two weeks in my tent. Mostly because of rain. Rain and constant and persistent wetness. It was a long but, oh so restorative, two weeks.

When the rains first began, I was on a hike and dripping wet before I made it back to the only market, if it could even be called that, in the Park. Bringing rain gear apparently escaped my mind all those months before when I was packing – big bummer! The market supplies were limited, and I was out of luck. No rain gear for me.

The next store was hours away by vehicle. I wasn't so quickly defeated, though. I bought a big black trash bag and cut a hole in it for my head and arms. The most important parts were covered, my backpack and gear. I'm sure I looked like a complete idiot, but that kind of crap never bugged me; I had had the title many times before! At least I gave the staff a good laugh. And they could laugh all they wanted. I felt like a genius, dry, underneath that silly looking get-up.

Unfortunately, my black-bag fix did nothing for my feet. My hiking boots were soggy for weeks, which wreaks havoc on the skin of your feet. Not that there was any comparison, really, but it made me think of soldiers suffering from "trench foot" in Viet Nam or the World Wars. Nasty stuff.

But worst of all was the state of my tent and sleeping gear. I'd stuffed socks in the corners of my tent when the rain started, because the fly didn't quite cover the whole thing. After a few days of nonstop rain, I had no more dry socks. Which really wouldn't have made much of a difference because of my perpetually sodden boots.

But then the water level started rising and my sleeping space became more cramped, if that were even possible in the already-tiny confinement of my Clip Flashlight tent. The National Park is at elevation, and it wasn't exactly warm at night to begin with. Add one soggy human to the mix, and it was downright miserable at times. Shivering all night with the only hope of reprieve being sunrise. If you've ever been cold and wet in a tent, you understand how desperate the situation seems the hour before the sun rises. Ugh! My one and only book had turned into a sponge with words. It became a kind of game to see how many pages I could actually read at night with my flashlight hanging over the nicely sodden paper. Luckily, the ink didn't run!

The story was of a woman traveling through the Galapagos Islands, and reading it made me feel like I had a friend there in the tent with me. We were sharing our travel stories and becoming pioneering sisters of sorts, the two of us. The rain was not going to get the best of me! I hung in there, went hiking every day wrapped in my trusty black trash bag, and persevered in reading my sodden sponge when darkness fell. All I really wanted was to sit by a warm fire. It's a love/hate relationship sometimes, being in the outdoors. I may have hated the cold and wet, but I loved every minute of camping in the Tasmanian national park. Weird, but as any outdoorsman(woman) can attest to, very true!

There's a connection that comes with being completely alone in a natural setting. The discomfort of my situation made me appreciate everything in my life on a deeper level. Like I needed to be completely stripped of my mind's understanding of external needs in order for my soul to emerge again. To shine again. Let go of the partying, the drugs, the alcohol, the cigarettes. I hadn't had a beer in over a week! In that sodden little tent somewhere in the middle of the Tasmanian forest, I became whole again. And it felt phenomenal. Soggy and chilled to the bone, and phenomenal!

When the time came to head out of my trusty little campsite in search of broader pastures, or whatever lay ahead, I once again found myself on the side of the road, all my belongings at my feet, with my thumb out. The passengers in the thoroughly packed station wagon that picked me up made for a very enthralling next few days!

***

"We meet the people we're supposed to when the time is just right."
- Alyson Noel

I came to calling them the "Energy Group." Danny, a holistic practitioner from Wisconsin; Robin, a self-proclaimed Merlin of Australian background; Faye, his very submissive healer wife; and Ben, Faye's awkward teenage son. When Robin pulled the station wagon over to give me a lift, I took one look and wasn't sure where I would fit. It was crammed full of shit and four people. But we made it happen. Once my pack and I were stuffed into the milieu, we were off. Out of the four people already in the car, not one of them asked where I was headed. Just the normal chatter of fellow travelers meeting.

"Where are you guys headed?" I asked after squishing my belongings and myself into the tiny space available in the back seat.

"Going to see some caves not far away," was the simple, no-frills answer.

And so it was. I not only joined them on their caving excursion, but spent the next three days with this odd, yet quite entertaining, group. At the end of the day, we landed at the campground where my adventure began and set up camp together. I found the whole scene extremely amusing. I just appeared out of thin air to join their little ensemble, and suddenly I was part of the mystical, magical group.

When I say Robin was a self-proclaimed Merlin, there was really no other way to put it. He even looked like he was right out of a science fiction film. Picture this: tall, black, lace-up boots; black pants with a tucked-in, puffy-sleeved, linen shirt; long, gray goatee and a medium length ponytail of grayish-brown hair; rings on almost all of his fingers; and to top it off, yes, he actually wore a black cape which tied loosely around his neck. A fucking cape, no lie!

Faye fit the part perfectly. She was tall and too thin, with frizzy hair, walked with almost a slouch, spoke in a very muted tone with her head slightly hung, wore a long flowy skirt, and lots of shiny jewelry. Ben, her son, was about fifteen or sixteen I would guess, very quiet, wearing all black, tall, also too thin, and soft-spoken. I say, "her son" and not "their son" because never once did I hear Ben address Robin as Dad. It was always Robin. Faye and Robin were not married, and I got the feeling theirs was a somewhat new relationship. And that could get interesting.

Danny, on the other hand, was the opposite of the others. He was a very rotund, somewhat short, man with a loud voice, prematurely bald for his middle age. He wore jeans and a t-shirt. Such a captivating and peculiar bunch they all made! I wondered how I fit in among them. How to describe myself? Young, carefree, slightly pudgy, American hitchhiker with backpack, ripped shorts and t-shirt, who hadn't showered for a few days too long. Ha!

I had been waking up in the mornings with really puffy eyes, and Danny did some energy work on me to help alleviate the condition. In one of our sessions, he said I had a lot of turbulent energy stuck in my solar plexus area (right around my midsection) that needed to be moved. That night I had a dream that I was walking through a waterfall of dark green water, very vibrant and alive. The next morning, no more puffy eyes! Very cool indeed!

Robin and Faye seemed to thrive on bickering. No, I'll change that to complete passive aggressive behavior towards each other, sometimes over-reaching the "passive" level through all-out screaming matches. Robin was a bit of an asshole, and Faye was a complete pushover. Not very evolved beings, as it turned out, despite all the frivolity of their external appearances. Poor Ben was just trying to get through his teenage years with idiots as parental figures. It didn't seem to be going too well for him.

Although I wouldn't exactly call them my best friends and the scene was more than a little bizarre, it was a welcome change to have people around to enjoy the outdoors with. The rain had stopped by then, and we all took a few hikes together, gathered around the campfire at night, and had some, um, interesting healing sessions, to say the least!
These characters were wonderful entertainment, anyway.

It's always helpful to me to put things into perspective when compared to other people's lives. These guys made me feel completely and utterly normal. Now that's funny! A few days into our time together, they packed up the station wagon and very matter-of-factly told me it was time they were off. On their own, without me. Allrighty then…

And I was back on the side of the road, sticking my thumb out. Life is divinely crazy!

Lisa Ruoff

***

Tasmania was beyond beautiful. After months of drinking, smoking, and partying, I had finally gotten a taste of the natural beauty of the continent. I did get the chance to visit more populated parts of this Australian state and learned that the island has quite the sordid and colorful history. Used as a brutal penal colony for convicts while it was still under British rule in the 18th and 19th centuries, many Australians never quite got over the unsavory reputation that came from that history. So, the story goes, the grim past of the island kept the current population low. Nobody wanted to live with such a black cloud over their heads.

    Two more nasty little secrets of the island were the mining and logging industries. Of course, this is coming from my perspective, and I was way more liberal than conservative. However, there had been conflicts between environmental organizations and the mining and logging conglomerates for years. From an airplane you would see the barren wastelands created by both industries, huge swaths of previously wild and beautiful lands and forests completely destroyed. It was heartbreaking, really, to see such devastation in such a stunning landscape. But every place has its ugly habit. Unfortunately, it didn't look like anything was about to change anytime soon.

My solitude during my time in Tas rejuvenated me from my core to my auras. But there were definitely times in that tiny tent, in the dark, wet, cold of night, that found me sleepless. Then my mind wandered to the experiences I had had in Australia so far. That incredible forest walk where I had the opportunity to get up close and personal with a few koalas who decided to come down and cross my path along their way to the next tasty gum tree leaves. Once again, similar to kangaroos, they're super cute and look adorably cuddly, but can realistically be nasty and inflict pain easily with their sharp claws and teeth.

And then there were the freakin' kookaburras. Arghhhh, the kookaburras!! Upon first hearing their very unique call, the magical newness wore off quickly. Their loud and obnoxious cackle was enough to make even the hardiest birders go insane after waking up to them every day for month upon month. And I, although a wildlife lover, am certainly not a hardy birder. They were everywhere, it seemed. No getting away from that distinct, witchy laugh. All of these first-hand experiences would float through my mind at odd hours of the night while lying alone in my isolated, little nylon abode.

But, more than anything else, my thoughts leaned towards my future trip to South Africa with Warren. The whole situation was really enough to make anyone go mad with anticipation. Having no immediate control over anything but the present moment, I had to let it all go. I had no other option but to just trust that everything would work out the way it was supposed to.

My heart ached from missing him. But I just couldn't give up this adventure. I had no explanation for him. I wasn't even sure how to explain it to myself. But did I really need to explain anything? There wasn't a day that went by that I didn't have him on my mind. But I wasn't willing to cut my trip short to run off to South Africa quite yet. I had to continue embracing with the greatest enthusiasm my daily adventures while trusting in the future. Easier said than done sometimes. I'd only a few weeks left before I would be back in Colorado again, preparing for our reunion.

***

*"Maybe it's just a daughter's job, to piss off
her mother."
–Chuck Palahniuk*

My mom was coming to visit me. Holy shit! This was absolutely earth-shattering news – for each of us. My mom and I had gotten along like oil and water for most of my life. Never seeing eye-to-eye on anything was a gross understatement. My father died about six years previously, and as far as I was aware, this would be the first international trip my mom was to take in at least thirty-five years without him, maybe the first ever on her own. I wasn't sure.

Our relationship had been almost non-existent since I dropped out of college and moved to Colorado a few years earlier. We just never got along, and it was too difficult for us to deal with each other. That was my perspective, anyway. And now, all by herself, she was coming across the globe to see me, her black sheep, wild-child, youngest daughter. Wow! I wasn't really sure how to feel about it. My emotions were all over the place. Anxious, trepidatious, honored, excited, scared. But mostly, I was intensely curious as to how it would go.

"You can't wear that," she said as she scanned me from head to toe with a mixture of repugnance and embarrassment.

"Well, Mom, sorry if I embarrass you, but you're just gonna have to deal with it," was my nonchalant reply to her apparent discomfort with me. I was no stranger to it.

There we were, standing at the ticket counter of the

Sydney Opera House. Me, happy and comfy in my ripped-up jean shorts and stained, body-hugging tank top. Let's just say that after six months of backpacking, my clothes weren't exactly starched and sparkly. And her, dressed in her usual proper casual attire, looking like she just might disintegrate from having to be associated with me. But neither of us had an option. If we wanted to see something at the iconic Sydney Opera House, the orchestra started in fifteen minutes. That left us with no time to go back to the hotel room and change. She was stuck with me the way I was.

With resigned acceptance, she bought the tickets, and we each had a surprisingly wonderful time, despite the bedraggled mess she considered me to be. The night was phenomenal! The Opera House was a gorgeous site to behold. And then the orchestra began their rendition of Gershwin compositions. The multitude of orchestral instruments, played in perfect unity under such an awe-inspiring rooftop, were utterly magical. If you've never been in an opera house, a building specifically designed to make music sound as glorious as it can sound, you need to go. Put it on your bucket list. Buy tickets now.

I had never been inside an opera house before and was blindsided by the waves of emotion that overcame me during the performance. I didn't even know who Gershwin was.

Selections of his work formed the playbill that night. Honestly, I don't think it mattered which composers' music we were listening to. It transported me to another world. From euphoric highs to flowing tears, those notes carried me away. If I were to describe it in colors, it would be the most outrageous flow of aurora borealis ever seen. When the concert ended, my mother and I just sat, immobile and unspeaking, in our seats, clinging to the magic of the music and vibrant, flowing emotion just a moment longer. Coincidently, by then, the matter of my clothing had been long forgotten.

For our next adventure Mom and I went penguin watching. We learned there was a colony of little penguins that lived on the coast in North Sydney, at Manly Beach, not too far away. Really, Australia had penguins! Super cool, right?

They're called fairy penguins and only grow about a foot tall. Little mini penguins! There we were with a bunch of other voyeurs, all lined up along a makeshift boardwalk in the sand, to catch a glimpse of these adorable mini tuxedo clad birds. At sunset, they would make their way back from foraging for food in the ocean all day. They did not disappoint. Just as the light started to dim, they came waddling up from the surf in sizeable groups, for best protection, we were informed.

We had been strictly warned that this was a spectator sport and we were not to interfere, in any way, with

Mother Nature in all her glory or gruesomeness. You see, being so small made the fairy penguins a delectable item on the menu of many predators. The mom and dad penguins left their burrows each morning, with the littlest of little penguins being left behind for the day. By sunset, they made the trek back up the sandy beach to their young waiting in the burrows. It was definitely a high-stakes game, trying to outsmart the predators in order to keep the kids alive.

If they were lucky enough to live through the seals, sharks, and other sea creatures, they had to deal with all the flying menaces – hawks, seagulls, and pelicans. Since they built their burrows into the dunes along the southern beaches, there were also threats on land, including dingoes, cats, dogs, even the careless obliviousness of humans. We watched until it was too dark to see.

It broke my heart to think of how much, strength, stamina and primal drive was required of these little treasures of nature to make it within feet of their burrows only to be snatched by a seagull or to have their young crushed by unknowing human feet.

An audible, yet muted cheer could be heard for every couple of parents that made it back to waiting babies. We were honored to have been witnesses. What an incredible world we live in! And, at the same time, how vulnerable to the vagaries of Darwin's Law of the Fittest, made more complicated by encroachment on habitat, introduction of non-native species, and the like. Unfortunately, in the present year of 2023, the Manly Beach colony is on the "threatened species" list, with less than sixty breeding pairs remaining, where there were hundreds in 1995.

***

On the lighter side, along the lines of "I couldn't make this up," there was the night I left Mom to her own devices while I went out partying with a friend in Sydney. It was only supposed to be a drink or two. Honestly. Alas…I don't have a very clear recollection of the exact events, but I do remember banging on the hotel door at about 3:00 am, yelling for Mom to open up because I couldn't find my key. To which the reply came from about four rooms down the hall where her blurry head was sticking out the doorway, "I'm down here," was all I heard.

My confused, slurred reply was, "What are you doing down there?" I don't think it was a proud parenting moment for her.

I'm not sure how long I was banging on the wrong door. Silly drunk girl. Oops! Mom was not amused, to say the least. The next morning found me ridiculously hung over, and Mom had taken leave of my company to take a self-tour of Sydney. I was impressed! Go, Mom, go! As usual, she forgave me for my foolishness, however grudgingly. Thanks, Mom.

She drove me crazy. I drove her crazy. Just like we had been doing since I was born. Just like we will continue to do, most likely, for the rest of our lives. We have never agreed on anything. Both of us are completely confounded as to how or why we are mother and daughter. There's no bond there, and very little connection. But there is blood.

I am her daughter and she is my mother. I don't have to like her, and I certainly don't understand her (and vice versa, I'm more than sure)! Still, I have always loved her and always will. There are people that hold on to what they perceive as the wrongdoing of their parents for their entire lives. Blaming and accusing always seemed to be such a waste of time and energy to me. Of course, there were times that I went through those emotions myself. But growth is about taking personal responsibility. And, as an adult (sometimes, anyway), I was trying to take responsibility for my life and my own actions. God knows, they weren't what my mother would have chosen for me! Whatever issues I had with my mother I honestly did not believe she did anything consciously to hurt me.

Over the years, I have come to learn that we just spoke different heart languages. I was always looking for hugs, I love you's, and some sort of pride in me, as her daughter.

But that's not the way she showed her love. Never has been.

She was always more pragmatic in her way of loving. Her door has been and will always be open to me. And should I ever find myself in a bind, her hand will always reach out. Just because her love wasn't presented in the form I was looking for, it was – and is – still there. She blames her gray hair on me and my wildness, and she has a valid point in that! Ah… Mother/daughter relationships… Job security for therapists throughout the ages.

We are all human, even our parents. Some people never understand that. For Mom and me, at the very least, we ended our week together with some heartwarming memories. I believe that each of us was surprised and humbled by what a pleasant time we had meandering around Australia together.

And that was that. Mom went back to her secure and comfortable life in New Jersey; my six-month adventure in Australia had come to an end, and I was sad to be leaving. Many friends acquired, many parties enjoyed, many adventures experienced, and oh, so many memories made!

Maybe I should have been feeling nostalgic and reminiscent, but really, I felt fulfilled and content and was ready to be moving along. That crying girl on the beach from six months ago was not quite a different person, but a much more grounded and secure individual (although, admittedly, with a somewhat abused liver). I was proud of myself for being strong enough to make the adventure happen.

My travels in Australia were not undertaken to seek something or try to find myself. It wasn't a pilgrimage of any sort, external or internal. It was simply a need to travel. To see something new and get out of my comfort zone for a while. To open myself up to new experiences and get a different perspective of the world in some way. At least a different perspective than my old world. And I did. I felt great about it!

What I was unaware of at the time was that I had opened another portal in myself. The portal to wanderlust. Throughout my life moving forward, I would never be content with conventional normalcy again. Wanderlust shaped not only my present, but my future as well. Someday, I thought, I'll be back. But in the meantime, there is a big world out there. So much more to see and experience. And the thought of returning to Colorado to see my friends and family again, and then on to South Africa to be with Warren, was absolutely motivating and exhilarating. Onward!

Bite of the Travel Bug

***

The two months' time I had as a layover in Colorado, between Australia and Africa, was a whirlwind of energy and activity. As I was to come accustomed to, re-entry into the US and "real life" always takes some adjustment. Reentry does not go hand in hand with ease and grace. Although friends and family were happy to see me and enthralled with my travel stories, there was only so much that was acceptable before I was expected to just return to "normal."

The problem being there was no normal for me. Not anymore. Any wanderer can agree, we're in a league of our own. One that isn't understood by the world at large. Thankfully, I gave myself a mere two-month window to visit the world of normal. And then I would be free again.

Which meant I could jump around from friend to family member, sharing travel stories and revelry with just enough time and just enough family and friends to regale, enjoy, move on to the next hospitality suite, and repeat. In that time, I did a bit of work, saved up a teensy bit of money for the upcoming Africa adventure, and touched base with people close to me. But more so, I decompressed after the intensity of Australia, equalized to the real world, and started planning for the next adventure. I was so excited to see Warren again that my plans, such as they were, really focused only on securing my travel visas and purchasing the airline ticket. Once I got there, we would resume being us and strive towards happily ever after. Oh, the naïveté of youth!

Africa

"Love has reason that reason cannot know."
—Blaise Pascal

The French are notorious for being arrogant and rude but, thankfully, that was not my experience. My nineteen-hour flight from Denver to Cape Town had a twelve-hour layover in Paris, and I wasn't about to miss my opportunity to taste at least a tidbit of the "City of Love." Back then, in 1995, it wasn't such a pain in the ass to come and go from an international airport, but that didn't mean I wanted to sit in one for a dozen or more hours. I had checked my backpack as baggage, so no worries about lugging that around. The few francs my sister, Lynn, had given me from her international money stash would be enough, I hoped, for the basics without needing to exchange dollars. (Yes, this was still the era of francs before the all-inclusive Euro.) And so it was, with no knowledge of the French language, and not a clue as to my whereabouts or how to get around, I ventured out into the romantic, pompous, absolutely exhilarating, city of Paris.

I stood on the tarmac just outside of the airport exit, utterly confused and more than a bit trepidatious, yet stubbornly determined. Lost in a sea of busses and taxis, a lone Italian-looking woman, with breasts threatening to break out from their cotton imprisonment, took pity on me and pointed me to the correct bus. I guess I had "confusedAmerican-looking-for-a-cheap-bus-to-wonderful-Parisiantourist-destination" written all over my face. Following her recommendation of bus routes, I jumped on board and waited expectantly for my adventure to begin. Really, for a few minutes, my only thought was that no matter what happened, I just had to find my way back to the airport within the next seven or eight hours. In the meantime, be open to whatever else lay ahead.

The sights of the city quickly transformed my apprehension to excitement. How can one remain anxious as they're passing the Arc de Triumph and Notre Dame on a public bus in Paris? A few gracious passengers gave me tips along my way – "This is a good stop for the Eiffel Tower, right around the corner," or "The Louvre is just two stops away." I even got a free ride on a shiny, red, double-decker bus from a Mauritius-turned-Parisian tour guide with smoldering, mocha-amber eyes who seemed to enjoy my company.

Unfortunately, the Louvre was closed on Tuesdays (guess what day it was). But that didn't stop me from taking a quick walking tour of the square that housed the Louvre entrance. The iconic glass pyramid that rises from the ground, inviting guests to enter from lands near and far (on every day but Tuesday) loomed large in my presence, and its magnificence humbled me. If the entrance made me feel inconsequential, I couldn't imagine the effect experiencing the treasures of the world's most visited museum would have had!

I quickly learned that everything costs money in Paris. Including the bathrooms. As it turned out, I didn't have enough francs for both the bus system and the public toilets. Ever resourceful, I found myself hiding in the thick bushes under the Eiffel Tower. There's only so long Mother Nature can be ignored and fortunately for me, tourists were scarce that afternoon.

Since my plan didn't really include a day in Paris, and I hadn't changed over any money, this visit would not include the partaking of local wines while savoring a fresh croissant at a quaint café on an iconic cobblestone street, though that's still on my bucket list. All in all, I had a fantastic day enjoying the magnificent and historic city of Paris, and I am proud to report that the Parisians I came across did not live up to their reputations.

As I relished the excitement and beauty and romance of

Paris, my heart and my head could not help but thrill to the very real and imminent possibility of spending my life with Warren. After eight long months, we would be reunited. And one day we would come to Paris. I could not wait to look into his beautiful blue eyes again and squeeze him tight in a long overdue hug. There wasn't a day that had gone by that I didn't think of him or wonder about our future together. All those months in Australia and then back in Colorado wrapping up the life that I knew. And here I was, so close, almost there in his homeland of South Africa, with him. Just one more continent to fly across and I would be there. In just a few short hours. The anticipation was almost unbearable.

I embarked on this nineteen-hour flight and twelve-hour layover in Paris with complete uncertainty as to what – or who – was going to meet me on the other side. You see, being the era before cell phones, texts, or social media, we had to rely on good old phone calls and emails. Add to that the fact that both of us were pretty much homeless, crashing with different people here and there. Our mutual lack of stability did not bode well for strong communication. I will also add, as with most men, Warren's communication skills, on his best days, hovered somewhere around appalling.

So, there I was, disembarking from an extremely long and tedious journey across half the globe, and Warren was, in fact, there to meet me! The man for whom

I had gone to such lengths actually honored our relationship by greeting me upon arrival, and it meant the world to me. He was there! That one hug felt like an unspoken novel. No words. Just our hearts trying to get as close as physically possible. It seemed to last forever and, at the same time, somehow ended much too soon. Such an enormous release of feelings after almost eight months of clinging to "us" via long distance! The uncertainty I had felt just minutes before melted away in that hug. Once again, our future radiated love and hope. God, how I adored this man!

For five days, I was happily delusional. Believing that we were on the right track. Putting things back together again and working towards making our connection solid. Sharing our love for each other and turning our focus towards our future. I was young and in love and invincible. It was all going to be fabulous, Warren and me. Maybe not without its pitfalls. But we would deal. Look at what we had gone through already. Eight months of being apart and here we were, solid as ever. Our love obviously had stood the test of time. My heart was full.

He was sharing a flat with his good friend Kate, and we had our own room. Although it had been five days of sleeping next to him without so much as a kiss, we would cuddle and talk about what we missed from the other's life in the last eight months. Sharing stories and getting reacquainted once again.

Whereas once we couldn't keep our hands off each other, we did not rush into each other's arms, all hot and passionate. We were taking it slow. I didn't really know why. Slow was not at all what I had envisioned. But I trusted we were heading towards a place of greater closeness, physically and emotionally. I was just so happy to be with him again.

"It's been eight months," I told myself. "It'll take some time to feel intimate again," I reasoned. We were going to be perfect. Not a doubt in my mind. We simply needed more time together, to just be together.

And in that spirit, with Warren as my guide, we explored the artsy and bohemian area known as Observatory, just outside of downtown. We took our time and leisurely perused the market stalls and boats of the waterfront. And we enjoyed a few delicious Black and Tans along the way.

In those simple joys, I remembered all the reasons I loved this man to my core. And I felt extraordinarily special to finally share in his love for his birth country and home. I was so carried away I performed a divine act of devotion – washing his jeans by hand, which was a huge pain in the ass. There was no washer or dryer in the flat. I hung them to dry at the café where Kate and I met while Warren was at work. The pampering housewife was never really my gig, but that day I was beaming, feeling like such a considerate and loving partner.

"God, I feel so in love! I'm just so fucking IN LOVE!" I gushed to Kate over coffee that morning. And she just joined in on my happiness. Even so much as stating how wonderful it was for her, as his best friend, seeing him so happy. For those five days, I was the eternal optimist. We were the perfect couple. Together, we would step into our future. My mind was figuring out how it would all look.

I would find work in Cape Town. Maybe we would explore getting our own place sooner than later, and we would start the next chapter of our lives together. Sure, there were moments that were awkward, maybe even uncomfortable. But I overlooked them. Wrote them off as inconsequential, or just misperceptions on my part. I was way too obsessed with the grandeur of our future together to notice anything askew.

Then, after five glorious days that felt like the beginning of a new world for me, he dropped the bomb. How he got through five days of that sham, I will never understand. The conversation started with me being extremely confused about the shift in energy, and he was like a dog that just got caught eating the holiday turkey off the table. If he had had a tail, it would have been between his legs.

"I'm in love with someone else," he said. He tried to keep talking, but I just sat there, hearing nothing more than those first six words. Within the few seconds it took for my brain to comprehend what they meant everything just went numb.

And then the understanding came to me. The dawning of the end of my world. It wasn't even pain, those first few moments, more like numbing shock. I couldn't breathe. It was a feeling more akin to standing on top of the earth as it split open under my feet due to a massive earthquake. It was confusion. Like all of the sudden he wasn't speaking a language I could understand. And then the reality of his words somehow hit me in my place of absolute knowing. I was simultaneously terrified and crushed. There was a crack in the earth. Just my earth, not his.

Somewhere in the wake of the aftershock of all hose tumultuous feelings, I was able to make out some more details from his words.

It had been going on for a month. A freaking month?! But, wait, he knew I was coming to see him a month ago.

It was his best friend's wife. How fucking cliché of him. She was fifteen years his senior. So, he jumped into bed with his best friend's wife once he found out I was coming to be with him? Jesus, my mind was reeling...

But the real kicker – the one that finished me off was that she had a baby. No. Not just any baby, but a baby that was the same age as ours would have been. The one that we decided together NOT to have. Yes, that age. He said he felt an overwhelming spiritual connection to this child that he simply could not ignore.

"WAIT!" my mind screamed. "We made that decision together. We walked that path together!" He was at the clinic with me, holding my hand, sitting with me after the "procedure," as we called it, wrapping a blanket around my legs. It was our decision. We were too young. We weren't ready for that kind of responsibility. It would have been totally unfair to that child. But, in his world, he was obviously being given a second chance. Just not with me.

Like I didn't matter. Like somehow our pain, our loss, suddenly became his karma. Like my role in that scene had just gotten cut. Like going through all of that emotional hell, as a couple, never existed for him.

Jesus Christ, it was like a kick in the gut. Like a woman doesn't carry that decision with her every single day of her life. But just in case I hadn't, there it was. In. My. Face. Another excuse to churn up all those exhausting emotions again. How could you, Warren? How could you do this? To ME? It hurt so bad. I felt I was being eviscerated all over again. This was so beyond "Ouch!"

A driving factor in his decision to be with this other woman was that she had given birth to the baby that he thought should have been his (ours). That thinking was so beyond wrong in my mind, I couldn't grasp it. In some weird, twisted, fucked up way, I was supposed to take some responsibility for this, too? Absolutely not. Nope, I would not let him pawn this off on me. I refused to be dragged down that road again. Especially with someone who was showing himself to be so completely and unabashedly selfish, cruel, and self-absorbed.

He said once he knew I had gotten my plane ticket, he'd broken it off with her. He still loved me. He was confused. He just needed some time. And on, and on, and on. And I, being young and naïve, thought that meant I still had a chance.

It seemed like an eternity. But it was really just about a week. A week of back and forth. A week of him disappearing to the other woman. A week of his friend Kate trying to console me. Of my heart being torn apart, piece by piece. A week of delusion before I realized I was being had.

So, I had a chance, did I? A chance at what? At getting back a man who had no problem crushing me? No problem lying to me? No problem deceiving me? A man who couldn't pick up the phone, send an email, or even write a "Dear Jane" letter by hand and send it via international snail mail? A chance for a man who had no balls?

He was a fucking bastard and I hated him for it. Molten anger seeped into the cracks and crevices of my shattered heart. I knew I hadn't been the most loyal of girlfriends. I'd had my fun down under. I never asked him about his actions. It was an unspoken treaty – this was our separate time to do what we needed. We were taking a break after two years together in Colorado. The deal was that once we met up again in South Africa, when and if we made it that far, we would be together.

He breached that contract. He let me come all the way to Africa, KNOWING that he had doubts about us. Knowing that his heart was torn. Knowing, knowing, knowing he was conflicted. But not brave enough to share the truth with me. Beforehand. My Warren was a fucking coward. He may not have outright lied to me, but he was less than forthcoming and that's a very fine and perilous line to walk.

I trusted him. I believed in him. What happened to the complete and utter honesty between us? Sure, he was afraid to tell me, but fuck fear. I deserve better. And I will not take crumbs. So, spare me your angst and your apologies and your nauseating bullshit. Enough, you confused, selfish asshole. ENOUGH! Fuck you, buddy.

I wished him the best of luck with the other woman. He was going to need it. She was going to need it, too. I mean, what new mother has an affair with her husband's best friend? And fifteen years her junior, no less? With a one-year-old baby involved? Isn't she concerned that one day Warren might run off with HER best friend? And isn't he concerned about how seamlessly she exits one relationship for another? They have no scruples. Neither of them. As far as I was concerned, they deserved each other.

I know, I know. Life is messy. Love is messy. Anger festers and destroys the soul. Forgiveness is the answer. But I was not there yet. If I were able to reach the place of compassion, perhaps I would embrace the truth that "love has reason that reason cannot know." But in the meantime, he could go fuck himself. And she could rot in hell.

And thus, my African adventure began. I had little money, no friends or family even remotely nearby, and I was a complete emotional and physical wreck.

Little did I understand then, but a myriad of men in my future would be paying the price for Warren's choices and their impacts on me. To say I was broken-hearted would be a gross understatement. I was inconsolably crushed. Devastated. Torn to bits and left to rot. Although there was nothing visibly wrong with my physical form, besides my puffy, swollen eyes, my insides felt like they had been mixed in a blender at high speed. Most specifically, my heart. Up to that point in my young life, I thought I had been in love a few times, but apparently, I was mistaken. This feeling was unlike anything I had experienced thus far. Nor cared to ever again. Whoever said, "Our hearts break to make room for new love," was full of shit.

It mattered little that I was inconsolable because I was in a foreign country and had no one to console me, even though I wanted it. The gods, however, showed me some mercy. I was able to procure a safe, secure, and most importantly, free, place to stay while my heart mended sufficiently to enable to me to leave the protection and solace of my bed to rub a few brain cells together.

The parents of Laura, a girl I worked with in Australia, lived in the area. In a true show of sisterhood, she reached out to them to ask for their help. When they learned my predicament, they graciously offered me a week or two of safe harbor in their basement. There I was, grief-stricken and broken-hearted in a stranger's basement in Cape Town, South Africa. So much for the beginning of my happily-ever after.

After the "fallout," my little basement refuge in Cape Town was a Godsend. Although I was a heartbroken, deserted wreck of a woman, that place gave me the security and space to just be miserable and pathetic for a bit.

It took about a week or so before I had to don my "big girl panties" and rejoin civil society. I gave much gratitude to my friend's parents for their enormously generous hospitality and off I was on the road again with my monstrous turtle's shell strapped to my back. Not that it was getting any easier to get the shell on and off, but repetition made it more manageable. And, I figured, in the long run, it would strengthen me, right? Or kill me.

One or the other, but either way, I had to get moving. No matter how much time I spent as a sodden pile of disintegrated compost on the floor of that basement apartment, it would not change the fact that I had been dumped. And it hurt. And it was going to hurt for a long time. A lot longer than even I knew, but that's another story, entirely.

This storyline: I was in Africa. My original plan was to be with Warren, the supposed love of my life, and live happily ever after. Due to the most absolutely unforeseen circumstances, my dance card was now wide open. As I saw it, I had some options. I could just tuck tail and retreat to
Colorado or I could get out there and add to my worldliness.
In other words, remain in Africa. Not really a hard choice, actually.

Once I allowed myself to peek out into the big world of possibilities, my good old friends – wanderlust and intrigue – overpowered my depressive state and filled my head with their warm, fuzzy security blanket of ideas and possibilities. Kate had taken pity on me and extricated me from my basement dwelling to a nearby town called Stellenbosch for an afternoon.

A university town surrounded by mountainous terrain and numerous vineyards, it felt like home instantly. It would be the perfect place to find some work and hunker down for a while, if that's what I wanted, to work. With enough money for at least a month or more, I wasn't so sure. But employment in a vineyard outside of a university town in the mountains close to Cape Town certainly was appealing.

One of the vineyards we visited was home to a flock of waddling, quacking, pooping ducks employed as voracious devourers of vine-eating bugs, as well as direct producers of natural fertilizer. Impressively sustainable. However, adventure called. And the countless opportunities awaiting me far outweighed returning to work right away.

There was a flyer on the bulletin board of the hostel I'd recently moved to, advertising a twenty-three-day kayak trip down the Zambezi River, just east of Victoria Falls and along the border of Zimbabwe and Zambia.

Of course, this was the most appealing choice – kayaking through crocodile and hippo-infested waters, while camping in lion territory on the riverside with a bunch of complete strangers and fellow (perhaps crazy, reckless) risktakers. YES - just what I needed to pull myself out of my "I've-been-dumped" blues!

And now for some interesting facts; the Zambezi River is a beast. At 1,559 miles (shall I round up?) it's the fourth longest river in Africa, the longest east-flowing river in Africa, and the longest river flowing into the Indian Ocean from Africa. Its basin drains 536,682 square miles, slightly less than the Nile River. The Nile is the longest river in Africa and considered historically to be the longest in the world, though some are contesting that status. New research suggests the Amazon River may be a touch longer.

I love waterfalls, their beauty, their power, their symbolism. As a Scorpio, being a water sign significantly influences my life. It may take some time, but water always wins! It will get through anything. Victoria Falls, for which the Zambezi is perhaps best known, is not just any waterfall. It's one of the Seven Wonders of the World and a World Heritage site. Of the world's waterfalls, Victoria Falls is not the tallest nor the widest, but it's classified the largest with a combined width of 5,604 feet and height of 354 feet, which is a mere 40-stories tall. These characteristics make it the world's largest sheet of falling water.

Other cool facts: It's found in two national parks and is visible from two countries, Zambia and Zimbabwe. Five hundred million liters of water, 132,086,026 gallons, cascade over the Falls per MINUTE – roughly equivalent to 200 Olympic-sized swimming pools. Impressive, right? But there is more.

Naturally, the interplay of sunlight and the Falls' water and mist create magnificent rainbows. But Victoria Falls is one of only two places in the world where "moonbows" occur – lunar rainbows formed when the light of the full moon hits the Falls. How utterly magical! I prayed we'd be there then. Lastly, the particularly daring can swim to the edge of the Falls (with a guide of course) at Devil's Pool. That's the ticket to cleansing me of my funk. But to do that, I'd have to swim ACROSS the Zambezi. Hmmm. What was it I read about crocodile and hippo-infested waters?

The trip didn't start for another few weeks, which would give me plenty of time to explore my way through South Africa and Zimbabwe and get to the put-in at launch time. I'd decide about the swimming bit later. Open to considering other potential adventures the Universe might place in my path, I decided to put the kayaking plan in my mind's mental parking lot where all potentially viable plans go, while I worked my way up to Zimbabwe. If it was supposed to happen, then it would. If not, I was starting to have faith in myself and in life again and knew that once I started traveling, something else just as fabulous and amazing would take its place.

The next few weeks consisted of making my way across the southern coast of South Africa, moving from hostel to hostel, meeting new people, and beginning the messy and challenging process of sewing together the pieces of my broken heart. I filled the days with enough adventure, travel, and new acquaintances that I had little time to obsess over Warren. Darkness seemed to go hand-in-hand with longing and heartache, and the forces were unrelenting.

Trying to sleep became a nightmare in and of itself. Even massive amounts of alcohol didn't help. As soon as I was left alone, my heart jumped right back up in my throat and demanded my full attention, and my tears would not be denied their time.

Over the weeks, my heartache turned to anger turned to bitterness. These emotional flows happened in the confines of my sleeping bag, usually in a room shared with at least ten others, under cover of night. Sometimes stifled sobbing, while other times muffled swearing and silent pillow punching. Fuck him.

Through all of this, often I would pull my tarot cards to try to receive some sort of other-worldly perspective regarding this whole bloody mess. I found a few mantras to ease my night troubles, and silently prayed to the Gods, Universe, Ancestors, Elements, and anything/anyone else I thought might help me over my devastation and sense of loss. And, of course, there was always alcohol and weed to dull the pain.

But no matter how hard I tried, it seemed that I just needed to allow my heart and my head to move through it all. Nothing would mask my pain or make it disappear or magically heal me. Ugh… In these moments I absolutely hated the revered concept of "personal growth." But then dawn would come and with it a new beginning. I would fill my time with adventure and busy-ness, and the evil night demons would rest and leave me in peace. For a bit.

"Travel is fatal to prejudice, bigotry, and narrowmindedness, and many of our people need it sorely on these accounts. Broad, wholesome, charitable views of men and
things cannot be acquired by vegetating in one little corner of the earth all one's lifetime."
–Mark Twain

While I was busy being self-absorbed in my emotional trauma, the larger world of South Africa was having its own problems. Nelson Mandela had taken over as President just a year before my arrival, and although this was an excellent turn of events for the native people of the country, it didn't come without its growing pains.

There were so many native tribes and languages that, in order to fairly represent the biggest portion of those, there were eleven official languages during those first few years of change. During the apartheid years, the white ruling class divided the people of the country by their original tribal languages. During my stay there, this was most obvious while watching TV. Every language was given one hour of air time.

Now, in 2023, those eleven languages still hold official status under the Constitution of 1996, but the majority speak either Afrikaans or English. Along with this mismatch of cultural tongues, there was much unrest in the country at large; understandably so after more than fifty years of apartheid. The undertones of hatred between the blacks and the whites were heavy. This affected me firsthand on one of my bus arrivals into a small coastal town.

I will leave the town unnamed so as not to incite judgement. It was one of my first stops along my coastal trek out of Cape Town, and I was excited to spend a few days in a non-touristy local area. As the bus made its stop, and I gathered my bags to disembark, I took a minute to look around and take in the scene. There was nothing specifically wrong. Nothing bad was happening in clear sight. But the energy emanating from the place, and the people, was actually sizzling with friction. And danger.

"DO NOT GET OFF THIS BUS," screamed the voice inside my head. Intuitively, I got it. It was not safe for me, specifically because of the color of my skin. Here, in these wonderful, beautiful, black-skinned peoples' minds,

I embodied centuries of suppression, hatred, and injustice done to them. And I couldn't find one ounce of reason to blame them. If I had their history, I would hate me, too.

As a white woman born into an upper-middle class family in New Jersey, USA, this was a first for me. My very first time being a minority. And reviled at that. The reality of my spoiled existence went down in a blaze of flaming entitlement. Millions of people throughout history have been killed, raped, tortured, and enslaved under the thumbs of my white ancestors. It was instantly and absolutely humbling, that single moment of realization on a public bus in a small coastal town in South Africa. A moment that has stayed with me for decades now and will continue to be with me until the day I die.

Every single person on this planet – especially rich, white people – should know what it feels like to be a minority. Every. Single. Person. We would live in a different world if that were the case. I did not get off the bus. I kept my entitled white ass right in that seat and kept on going. But those people, with such grief and loathing in their eyes, will remain in my heart forever.

Those few weeks held many adventures, mostly joyous. I learned that sandboarding is a real thing. Same as snowboarding, but on sand. Just like it sounds. Super fun and quite a workout, but MAN, watch out for the falling part! Falling off a board at high velocity onto granulated sand particles is like ripping your face off with sandpaper. Basically, it doesn't feel so good. Despite being a bit rough – literally – it was an exhilarating experience. The dunes were right on the coast, overlooking the Indian Ocean. It was an absolutely beautiful spot to be sandblasted!

Next, I rode horseback through a game reserve in the Drakensberg escarpment on the Lesotho border. Lesotho is a tiny country that lies right in the middle of South Africa. It is home to a few game reserves in what they call the Great Escarpment, an absolutely stunning high plateau area with jagged green mountain peaks rising up sporadically over the landscape. It was here I experienced my first African wildlife (besides those nasty baboons outside of Cape Town, that is). Zebras, wildebeest, kudu, elan, and giraffes, all viewed from the saddle of a horse. Phenomenal!

There really is no way to describe the feeling of running alongside a herd of giraffes while on horseback. No fences or gates. Just out in the open wild plains of Africa. I was giddy with excitement and appreciation. Giraffes are stunning animals, with their long necks, beautiful orangey-brown stripes, and gangly legs. Although they are enormous, everything about them is utter grace. They even run gracefully. We were told there were monkeys that lived in these plains, too. Apparently, none of them wanted to be seen that day. And the elephants didn't inhabit the area.

Later in my travels, I would see plenty of both.

My new friend, Sara, and I decided to go camping in the Drakensberg mountains for a few days. Our rendezvous point was a hostel in the huge coastal city of Durban. The bus system didn't offer any service in that region, so we had to resort to hitchhiking, and it turned out to be quite easy. As white women hitchhiking through a remote, mountainous region of central South Africa, there was no shortage of black men in pickup trucks willing to give us a ride. Although our driver wouldn't allow us to sit in the back of the truck. Which left us the only option of piling into the cab with two happy, smiling, young African men. Oh, they were so happy!

This might sound like a high-alert situation, but it was really very innocent. In stark contrast to my experience on the bus, the feeling here was very light and honest. Almost jovial. They wouldn't have hurt us any more than they would have hurt their grandmothers. But they certainly derived great joy in sharing a small space for a long drive. And we got a free ride to a stunning campsite at the base of some beautiful mountains in the middle of nowhere. Win-win.

Unfortunately for us, it rained most of the time we were there. Between keeping watch for thieving baboons, and playing cards, we stayed busy. The gods were kind enough to give us a reprieve for a few hours in the afternoon so we could enjoy some hiking adventures. At least we got some exercise and exposure to remarkable landscapes and habitat.

It was there, in those mountains, that I learned the word "mzungu," which I would hear countless times on my African trip. After a few wet days amongst a stunning backdrop, we packed up camp, stuck our thumbs out, and hitched another ride back to the hostel.

This time, an old African man with a face as black as night and teeth that seemed to illuminate when he smiled, picked us up, along with his happy canine sidekick. We were, fortunately, allowed to take the back, as the dog wasn't willing to share the cab with us, despite his friendliness. He simply refused to move out of the middle of the passenger's seat.

With all of his wagging butt and dog kisses, we were happily and agreeably forced to climb into the back. As we passed through a small village in the open truck bed of our hitched ride, the local school was letting out, and all the children were staring eyes wide, mouths agape, awestruck by our absolute whiteness.

"Mzungu! Mzungu! Mzungu!" they all cried out loudly and in unison, while pointing and running after the truck. When the truck finally stopped to drop us at our destination, we were able to ascertain, between the old man's native language of Afrikaans and our English, that "mzungu" translated to "white people." It seemed that they rarely saw white people in that area and were quite delighted to have the experience of our presence. We felt honored by their delight. Ah, the joyful innocence – and open-mindedness – of the young.

My travels were akin to an immersion program at a school for foreign languages. As such, my program was enhanced by witnessing a bonafide local "immersion" on a beach in the coastal town of East London. It was a glorious day. I was enjoying a gorgeous afternoon walk along the beach with a few friends from the hostel. Such a treat it was to feel the warm sand between our toes, and to have the beach almost all to ourselves. We'd been out for a while and were considering turning back when we rounded a bend and noticed a group of locals congregating around one area.

We were curious. As we drew closer, we saw that there was a man in robes, a pastor, it seemed, who was wading out into the water. He went out to about waist deep and was then followed by numerous presumed congregants who lined up, forming an aisle of five or six men and women on his left and right sides. Our small group of backpacking white foreigners was fascinated and couldn't take our eyes off the scene unfolding before us. Nobody seemed to mind that we were bearing witness; in truth, they hardly even glanced at us.

Lisa Ruoff

    Once the "aisles" were formed, each prospective baptism recipient proceeded, one by one, to wade into the ocean up to the pastor, receive a boisterous, spirit-filled blessing, and a full-on dunking in the salty sea. It seemed they had the blessing of the sea gods as well, due to the calm surf and lack of wind. The recently baptized reveled with abandon in the ocean, with much joy, merriment, and laughter. In my world, such carefree merrymaking would be considered sacrilegious during the rite of baptism. On land, the congregation drummed and sang and danced in simultaneous celebration.

    This was no somber affair. The entire spectacle was so far removed from my experience of religion. I won't subject you to the rationale for my personal disgust with organized religion. The blending of nature with God in the scene unfolding before me was new to me, surprisingly moving, and refreshing. It was quite apart from my memories of dark churches on Sunday mornings in somber settings where we worshipped an often-vengeful God. Yes, there was music, much of it beautiful. But this music was unlike any religious music I'd experienced before.

    What I was privileged to witness was pure rapture, freedom, and divine grace revealed through the joyful sounds and life energy that enveloped us, even though we stood on the fringes of the celebration. It brought ME joy, this disillusioned, lapsed, churchgoer, to see these beaming initiates happily dunked into the sea in the name of their God. I believe some of us mzungus were envious of the seaside baptism. To hell with the indoor baptismal font! I know each of us was honored to be present and thankful for the gift of this slice of spiritual life unknown to us before.

***

I never did make it to that kayak expedition down the Zambezi River. In fact, during the weeks of travel and adventure on my way through South Africa, I had forgotten all about the river trip and missed the launch date. For a moment, I was upset with myself. How could I have possibly forgotten about visiting the Seventh Wonder of the World? The prospect of experiencing a "moonbow?" The chance to swim to the edge of a fucking massive waterfall? Oops…

In my mind, after the appropriate self-flagellation, it just meant that it wasn't supposed to happen. Maybe I was going to be swallowed up by a river crocodile and this was the Universe's way of saving my ass. Who knew? Instead, I signed up for transport across the African continent on an overland truck, starting in

Zimbabwe and making a return trip to London. I learned of this option via hostel connections, and it made total sense to me and my wallet.

Typically, overland tours were destined for specific locations with specific itineraries, kind of like camping tours or safaris via truck. They were far from cheap! But this specific travel option was rarely advertised. After the tours are over and the final destination is reached, the truck still needs to wind its way back up to its original point of departure to start all over again. This is where entrepreneurial opportunity arises. The tour guides/drivers would post advertisements at local hostels in their end-of-tour town and make some extra money from cheap - I mean frugal - travelers who were basically looking for no-frills transport. The cost of this was less than half of the standard charge for scheduled tours. Count me in!

I arrived at 7:30 in the morning at this place called The Rocks in Harare, Zimbabwe, to climb aboard. As usual, African time held true and by 10:30 am, the truck still hadn't arrived. In the meantime, the ten of us who chose this particular means of transport began to get acquainted.

Regular tours accommodate up to thirty "guests." With only ten of us, we had ample room to spread out. After only a few weeks on the truck, I wondered how the hell thirty people crammed in the back would have found any enjoyment. While wandering the gardens and rocky outcroppings of the aforementioned "Rocks" waiting for the elusive transportation to arrive, I met Pippa. A right proper Englishwoman, she was. (I always was a fan of the British way with words.)

Neither of us knew it at the time, but we would keep each other company through some pretty crazy shit in the coming months. As was usual for most Europeans after university, Pippa was taking a year off to travel and see some of the world. I can't recall why she specifically chose Africa, but unfortunately for her, she got to hear all about the misfortune that placed me there. Being the polite
Englishwoman that she was, she listened to my sordid tales of Warren and his utter and egregious lack of genuine compassion and empathy. And oh, how could I forget, loyalty, honesty, and decency? God love this woman.

Then there was Derek, the endearing, mammoth, goofball of an Australian who soon became our muse. Derek, Pippa, and I became the Three Musketeers (or Three Stooges given the tenor of the day). The inseparable, happy, traveling trio. Just three solo, endlessly inquisitive adventurers who were fortunate to find each other in the wilds of Africa.

Oh, and I had so much to be thankful for. Those two were endlessly patient with my repetitive, dramatic, depressive rantings about that horrid human being, Warren, and my pitiful, broken heart. Seriously, they were saintly. We were destined to meet up then and there, while waiting for an elusive truck to take us to mysterious and unknown places.

After another hour of waiting around and getting to know each other, the truck finally appeared. Could this monstrosity possibly be a truck? We heard it before we saw it, and for a minute, I thought we were under siege. The thunder of the engine simply engaging into low gear, and the overly loud clinking and clanking of numerous unknown metal parts preceded the entrance from around the corner of an immense, ugly, tan-colored beast of a box on enormous wheels, taking tree limbs out along its turning axis.

They called it an overland truck, but the closest thing that came to mind was those off-road rigs used by the National Guard in the event of disasters such as monumental flooding, earthquakes, or tornadoes. The vehicles that look like left-over inventory from WWII. From the ground up, I would guess our albatross stood about twelve-feet tall, and looked to be about thirty-feet in length (Twelve inches per person if the vehicle were at capacity? Eeesh!) The cab was separate from the back and could hold approximately four people comfortably. The seat outside, perched on the top, like a stagecoach, could similarly hold four. That stagecoach seat looked like prime viewing for just about anything (as long as we weren't going over forty mph, which was just about never)!

The back of the truck had roll-up canvas sides and bench seating along the side rails. The middle was open and quite spacious. In order to access the rear, there was a metal ladder welded onto the backside. Once up the ladder, the back "door," which was waist height, was easily clicked open and closed. The side "rails" were solid, so when seated you were leaning on solid metal like the bed of a truck.

Unless it was raining, the canvas siding was folded up while traveling for optimal viewing of the landscape and wildlife. The entire underneath of the truck was storage. Tents, cooking equipment, baggage, tools for possible repairs, extra gas tanks, and such, all had their own space under our seating area.

This thing was a behemoth. The truck of all trucks. The one truck to rule them all. It was beyond impressive. Extraordinary, really. I couldn't even begin to think of what terrible gas mileage it got! Luckily, that wasn't my problem to worry about. This massive pile of machinery would be home to me and nine others, for the better part of the next few weeks.

We all just stood speechless for a moment. My initial mortification was replaced with awe-struck appreciation. And then it was all chaos, as bags, camping gear, food supplies, and other miscellaneous items were shoved and crammed into the portals of the beast on wheels. By noon, we had all claimed our seats in the back and were on our way.

If you've never traveled through Africa by road, let me just tell you, it's not the fastest way to go. Riding a mule would have been faster. I can't account for how they are now, but back in 1995, even in and around major cities such as Harare, the roads were all dirt and ridden with potholes. Potholes that could have won Academy Awards for sheer size. Potholes that could house a family of six. They were enormous. And they were everywhere. I mean, every few feet. Of course, there were people, too. People with kids, with water jugs on their heads, pulling donkeys…And they, too, were trying to avoid potholes, so pedestrians and their whatnot were all over the road.

Add to this visual of normal traffic for the region and circumstances, and bear in mind "normal" or "regular" in this context has no relation whatsoever to American definitions or understanding of these words. Imagine Times Square, minus the high-rises, in the dirt, with no traffic lights. Add a bunch of aimlessly roaming animals, times a hundred. A kind of third-world Grand Central Station with motorbikes, taxis, small cars, trucks, donkeys, people, dogs, chickens, and of course, our beastly truck chugging its way through all the mess to try to make some miles towards Malawi, the next country of destination, hundreds of miles away.

It was a highly uncomfortable start of a long journey. But we were all young and happy to be on an adventure, and the jostling and jerking of the truck quickly became highly bearable, and soon we were inured. Because of the physical condition and crazy, unpredictable usage patterns of the roads, the truck could rarely drive at high speeds, (and what, really, is the definition of high speed)? As a result, we all took turns riding in the seats above the front cab. It was great fun to have such a prime view of the chaos and somehow made us feel connected with the people and animals in the milieu below. Absurd, absolute, beautiful, and all-encompassing chaos!

We quickly established a daily routine. Our drivers/guides were a highly likeable couple in their thirties, from Germany, Pim and Margo. They quickly schooled us in protocol. The return north to start another real tour, for real paying guests – which we were not – was their primary focus. We were mobile during the day and regardless of road conditions, we would strive to cover as many kilometers as we could in those daylight hours.

We, the passengers, got to sit around, enjoy the ride, and take in the sights. If conditions were right, we would switch out sitting in the seats above the cab. But if it was rainy, or the roads were actually good enough to go a decent speed (which didn't happen often), we were confined to the back. Although, with only 10 of us, the space certainly wasn't cramped. Once night fell, the drivers had the job of finding a spot to pull over that could accommodate the size of the truck and space for all of us to set up camp. Somewhere that was relatively safe, as well. "Safe" being a term of fluid definition given that we were in the middle of Africa, and subject to rapidly changing conditions.

Things-that-go-bump-in-the-night were completely different while camping on the side of the road in the middle of Zimbabwe than they were back in the States in a US Forest Service campground. Here, the animals were our worst threats and, as is usual protocol with all wild animals, if we were very careful about the food, we shouldn't have any problem with aggressive, hungry predator types. "Shouldn't?" I'd have preferred a decisive "wouldn't." Elephants, lions, water buffalos, hyenas, baboons – all of these animals were wandering around in the bushes of Zimbabwe at night, and we were taught to have a hefty respect for them and their space.

Tribal lands and the etiquette around passage through them or camping on them was another critical issue our trusty guides were aware of, but we were not. If we planned to camp on tribal lands, we had to ask permission of the tribal chief. In order to do that, you had to find the chief, obtain an audience with him, and secure permission. Basically, it was better to take your chances with a pride of lions looking for a meal. Needless to say, Pim and Margot tried to keep us off tribal lands.

After procuring an acceptable (and mostly legal) nightly campsite, one team of a few people would prepare the communal meal and clean-up. Another team would be responsible for setting up the tents and sleeping paraphernalia. These teams alternated daily.

Because we usually stopped at night, under the cover of darkness, we rarely knew our whereabouts until the next morning. One of those first mornings was among the most memorable of my life. From the bed of my little tent, even before my eyes were open, just as consciousness started to take over my dream state, I heard the sound of drumming. Off in the distance, but not too far from camp, very soft chanting accompanied the drumbeats.

I learned the beautiful sounds that slowly woke me from my slumber were a most unexpected gift from the nearby tribe drumming the sun into the sky. It was their way of welcoming each new day, to drum on their handmade djembes (typical African drums) and chant to the sun in welcome and gratitude.

There I was, in the middle of Zimbabwe, camped out in the bush, my location completely unknown, being awoken by the sound of indigenous peoples drumming and chanting their salutation to the new day. As with so many other times in Africa, I was awe-struck. I prayed I never tired of experiences like these. That such rituals never lost their power. How could you not have an absolutely amazing day after that kind of sacred awakening?

Every day, we followed the same routine, only backwards. Or maybe it was forward in the morning and backward at night? Hmmm... After everything was packed away and secured, we continued on down the road in our military-style, government-issued, security-grade, transport vehicle. Riding in the back as mere passengers was far from boring. As we quickly found out, we didn't need to be in a reserve park in order to see animals in their natural setting.

They were everywhere!

We viewed baboons not only swinging through the trees but behaving true to their reputations as big nuisances to people in the towns we passed. Those opposable thumbs really got them into trouble. And elephants – we even saw elephants! Just driving down the road, from the back of the truck, with nothing in between us but some rolled up canvas!

These were my first elephant sightings since I had been in Africa, and I was over-the-top elated. Giddy, really!

There were a few sightings of zebras, and lots of impala, antelope, and even a couple of kudus. Not that we spent much time enjoying them. The truck steadily forged ahead towards our destination. It didn't matter to any of us, though; we were all in animal-viewing heaven. There were even lions, but that's a story unto itself.

Every once in a while, the truck would have to stop for a night or even a few in order for Pim to take care of mechanical issues. During one of these stops, I decided I wanted to make some rice. But my camping stove, along with all the other kitchen equipment, was stored underneath the truck. Thinking I was having a brilliant idea, I decided to leave some uncooked rice, soaked in water, in my tin cup, in the sun for the day while we were freed from the truck for a while. It worked! When we returned, the rice had "cooked" sufficiently that it was soft enough to eat. Of course, I was all puffed up with pride at my amazing survival skills and ate it all up.

Within a few hours, we were all onboard again, and motoring at night because of our setback during the day. There was no bathroom on the truck, so whenever Mother Nature called, we would just bang on the solid barrier to the cab or holler out the window in the general direction of the driver. Cooking rice under the midday sun turned out to be not such a great idea, and I found myself banging on that barrier like my life depended on it. It seemed that some opportunistic bug had decided that my rice looked good and then I digested said bug unknowingly. Or some such hypothesis. Because I ended up with a brutal case of diarrhea while traveling through the wilds of Africa in the back of an overland truck with no bathroom. Oh, joy…

Derek and Pippa did their best to take care of me and to try to cheer me up, but there is really only one cure for such a problem. And that is to just go through it or, more literally, let it go through you. After many lurches for the barrier with a few good, swift bangs, and many climbs down the metal ladder to relieve myself in the bushes, and then back on board to hopefully sit it out for a while, the truck just stopped. I didn't remember hitting the barrier that time, but it happened so often that I couldn't be sure. Immediately, I jumped up, grabbed the toilet paper, and started down the back ladder. I was halfway down the ladder when I heard
Pim yelling from the driver's seat,

"Stay in the truck!! Don't get out!! And make sure everyone's hands and arms are not hanging out!"

For a split second, I was confused and torn. What to do? I wasn't really sure what was going on or why we had stopped, and Mother Nature was certainly calling. Yet Pim sounded pretty alarmed. So, I leaned over, while still mid-ladder halfway to the ground, and poked my head around the side. There, shining in the dark of night, were many pairs of glimmering eyes headed my way. A pride of lions had been lying in the road and the truck had startled them. They were on the prowl. A few more steps and I could have easily been on the menu! No time for thought, and no time for Mother Nature's calls. Back up the ladder I went, like lightning!

Somehow, I was able to hold my bowels until we resumed our trip down the road a bit. But for a good fifteen minutes or so, the ten of us got an up-close and personal introduction to a pride of lions on the hunt at night. There were five of them, all females, and all unquestionably regal in their predatory beauty. They seemed to be as interested in us and the vehicle as we were in them. They pawed around, glancing at us as they sprayed the tires with their scent, their eyes shimmering in the reflection of our flashlights. The pads of their paws were bigger than my hands, all spread out. And their coats were perfect, all groomed and beautifully golden tan in color.

My God, they were stunning. And they were just feet away. Human and lion, in a delicate dance of surprise introduction. I can't speak for the lions, but I know that every single human heart in that truck was pounding out of its chest that night. I gave immense gratitude to the Universe for allowing me this experience. My gratitude was especially profound because I wasn't part of the lionesses' feast. When I finally was allowed to heed Mother Nature's call, it was with great trepidation that I stepped off the truck and into the bushes!

Admittedly, even though I was still dealing with a severely broken heart, and I continued to burst into tears every few days from the memories of my recent breakup, there was a part of me that was eternally grateful to Warren. If it weren't for him, I wouldn't have been there. There was no reason on Earth that I would have traveled to Africa, and I certainly would not have been having these unforgettable, potentially once-in-a-lifetime experiences. My excursion through this profoundly foreign and beautiful land was more than I had ever imagined it would be, in part because I had not had to imagine it. My Africa vision had revolved around Warren, my love for him, our love for each other, and the potential for a long, happy, and purpose-filled life together.

But increasingly I sensed this journey would be truly life-changing for me in a variety of ways. In the depth of friendships, for example. Derek and Pippa were always there for me when I needed a shoulder to lean on or a tissue to dry my tears. Not to mention a good laugh now and then.

They had my back. There was no option really to dilly dally if I wanted to be safe and still experience the wonder of my surroundings. They listened but also limited my pity party time and happily pushed me forward to the next thing when I needed to get out of my own way, whatever that was.

I've known from a young age that other peoples' judgements of me were not my concern. And this was a good thing, a liberating thing. However, despite my staunch independence and my abhorrence of patriarchal society, when it came to opening my heart to another, I did need some approbation to validate my worth. The breakup with Warren revealed this in the clearest terms. And I hated it. The only consolation was that a) I now knew this truth, and b) I was simply too strong and independent of a woman for him.

But, as every human being does, I have needs for approval, especially given my family history. And when Warren was really real with me, I did feel whole. And that's what I missed.

Ah, but what a conundrum. Feel whole. How I dislike that phrase. That "you complete me" business makes me sick. I don't need anyone to complete me. I am enough.

This transformation began once I started trusting in the ebbs and flows, opportunities, and choices before me. It began when I ceased to dwell and wallow in the pain of the recent past. My heart and soul were coming back to life. To a new life overflowing with possibilities. To a place of gratitude, gratitude, gratitude. A truly grateful heart does not forget that there is nothing more precious than this day.

Lisa Ruoff

***

*"I love to see a young girl go out and grab the world by the lapels. Life's a bitch.
You've got to go out and kick ass."*
–Maya Angelou

Riding along in the back of our open truck, I began to feel a slow, but steady, integration of my being with the rhythms of local life. I was beginning to feel a part of the rich tapestry of sights, sounds, smells, and culture that were so unlike anything this Jersey girl had ever known. I was indeed venturing into new, undiscovered territory, and at the same time felt safe and protected in my special convoy, surrounded by English-speaking, white people my own age.

    I spent my days taking it all in. The furious pace of the cities was punctuated with cars, motorcycles, buses, trucks, bicycles; young people, old people, and people in-between; animals of all types, shapes, and sizes; established roadside markets, free-wheeling peddlers chasing down potential customers, and all the accompanying hubbub and chaos. The sounds alone were overwhelming! A cacophony that at times literally hurt my ears. Horns honking, people yelling, vendors hawking their wares through megaphones, dogs barking, brakes squealing, stereos blaring, engines revving – VROOOM! VROOOM! VRRROOOOOMMM!!.

And then there was the remoteness of the "bush," as it's called in Africa. Absolutely distinct from cities, it came with its own brand of chaos. Villages of thatched-roof huts, roadside bars – which were concrete block huts with holes as windows, usually frequented by drunk, skinny, local men dancing to very loud African music blasting from cheap speakers. Emaciated, stray dogs, communes of feral cats, local wildlife, both seen and unseen. Baboons were the ubiquitous patrons of both worlds, finding solace and pleasure everywhere – from tree limbs to garbage dumps to open kitchen windows (which were no different from the windows in the roadside bars – open holes in concrete walls). I learned to fear baboons much more than any of the four-legged riff-raff.

Both the city world and that of the bush were home to the ever-present aroma of burning trash. In Africa, there is trash everywhere. Everywhere. No exceptions. As you learn quickly, traveling in third-world countries, there is no such thing as throwing trash "away." It doesn't go anywhere. There is no away. No trash men magically show up in enormous trucks and pick up your trash from nicely sorted trash bins sitting on the curb in front of your beautiful suburban home. No sir, not in Africa.

Trash became part of my existence. It was always there to remind me that there was no "away." The stench of burning trash, all iterations of trash – compost, paper, tires, plastic, everything -- was etched in my memory for eternity. Even to this day, I can tell the difference between a trash fire and a wood bonfire. It's a smell that is burnt into a person's DNA, never to be forgotten, and somehow never quite to be enjoyed. Over time, my senses became immune to the stench. It may have just been my nose's way of clicking into survival mode; A few of my fellow truck passengers never got past the pervasive stink.

Another unsavory reality of everyday life on this continent was human excrement. As with trash, it was everywhere. Everywhere. Flowing in open ditches. Piled in alleyways. And, of course, free form behind the bushes at a seemingly perfect campsite.

Perhaps my most memorable encounter with shit was in Dar es Salaam when Derek, Pippa, and I were looking at a place to stay for one overnight. We asked if the room included use of a bathroom (often, cheap rooms did not). We shuffled to the back of the building behind our prospective host, and emerged into the alleyway behind the "hostel," where we had the privilege to view the water closet.

Two planks, precariously situated over a river of raw sewage, led to a hut with a door – because they held guest privacy of the utmost importance. The privy was simply a concrete floor with a hole in the middle. There were piles of human waste scattered around the floor of the hut, and I believe it goes without saying, the excruciatingly foul odor was enough to knock us all off our feet.

Actually, the schooling we received that night will stay with me for the rest of my life. Our African manager friend bitch slapped us in the face, figuratively not literally. Still, reminding us of a harsh reality we understand only remotely or in principle. I don't remember his exact words, but I will never forget the anger and disdain in his voice:

"You white people.... I fell for all of your empty words. I left my tribe, following promises of material wealth and opportunities. And this is where I'm stuck now. There is no such thing as a better life than what I had. My tribe won't take me back because I made the choice to leave for the outside world. Those promises were all just a bunch of lies. So how dare you turn up your nose in disgust?!" All of this was uttered under his breath and with complete contempt in our direction.

That is when I learned most African tribes leave the choice up to each individual, either stay or go. But if the decision is to leave, they are never allowed back into the tribe. If they chose to go, they were gone forever. Harsh... The truth of his words stung. He was right. Our white culture was full of worthless promises. I use the word "our" purposefully. I was part of that culture, whether or not I liked it. Honestly, that culture revolted me, but there wasn't anything I could do about it. Sorry, manager dude. I'm so sorry.

The bathroom situation described above was not at all uncommon in Africa. Even where there were bathrooms, it was good to be prepared. We always carried toilet paper with us everywhere we went. Derek, being a guy, had it a bit better than we who were relegated to squat. Necessity prompted innovation. Because of his colossal size, we quickly learned to use him as a human shield whenever needed and possible. Just hand him a sarong, and he became the best bathroom wall a girl could ever want. Derek was a professional at looking the other way! Bless him for his selfless service.

There wasn't much we could do about the horrific lack of sanitation in daily African life. It was deeply concerning from a public health perspective. It was beyond offensive to our delicate human sensibilities. But we had to learn to accept "the condition" unconditionally, while working toward a solution or supporting others to bring clean water and waste management to communities. If we could not detach through acceptance, we would be perpetually frustrated and our lives would be ruined by shit every day.

The poverty here was beyond overwhelming. The oppression seemingly insurmountable. The daily lives of the locals were dictated by what it was they had to do to survive. Trying to make sure they had enough food and water for their children to make it to tomorrow. Every day we passed countless women walking, with water jugs balanced on their heads, to and from water sources. It took most of their days just to get drinkable water! It was an existence that very few people in my life had any idea of, nor did they even want to know about, let alone experience firsthand.

Yet, somehow, the people of this African continent were usually happy. They could be found dancing and singing, pretty much anywhere you looked. The children, even though they lived in a constant state of hunger and malnutrition, were joyful and playful. The dichotomy of human spirit to human condition was blatantly apparent everywhere. It was a harsh, yet necessary, lesson for all of us on the truck to embrace.

Little did we know, but once we no longer had the protection of the huge, beastly, overland machine, we would all be out there on our own to handle these uncomfortable situations face-to-face. The Universe was slowly immersing us into the grit of African everyday life (mostly) gently and from a safe distance. We were all too clueless at the time to even be grateful.

One of our first overnight stops was at Lake Malawi at a camping hostel on the beach. The truck was having mechanical difficulties. As it took a few days to get the needed parts, we all camped out, drank, swam, and became acquainted with some crazy strong African weed called Malawi Gold, procured from Paul, the guy who ran the place.

He was a single, middle-aged, shirtless Brit, who always had a cigarette hanging out of the corner of his mouth, and a pack of dogs that seemed to follow him wherever he went. After three days at his place, and lots of beer drunk in his little lakeside palapa bar (open-sided thatched roof), none of us could figure out his story. And, unquestionably, there was a story. A man his age doesn't just decide to become an expat to the middle of nowhere in Malawi, serving lots of booze to traveling twenty-something-year-olds who happen to wander through, while taking on all the stray dogs of the village without a backstory. He never told us, and we had to live with the best our imaginations could conjure. But usually, the truth is crazier and wilder than anything my mind can dream up!

I pitched my trusty little tent in a small clearing near the lake shore, bought my own bag of Malawi Gold from a local guy, and promptly disappeared for the first twenty-four hours into a pot-induced coma. It was just crazy overload for my brain to handle the fact that every time I left the tent, at least ten local kids would come running from nowhere to scream "mzungu," grab one of my fingers (of which, all ten were accounted for by small, screaming beasts in seconds), hang onto me, swarm beside me, anywhere – and everywhere – I went. I had to shake ten kids off my fingers just to re-enter my tent in order to hide.

Mind you, this was my first experience face-to-face with local people for any length of time, while also being stoned off my rocker from their highly potent local weed. Whew! It was too much, and I wasn't ready, so into the tent it was for me. When I finally got the courage to deal with all the stimuli, I came to love it. Though the kids marveled at all of us on the truck, some were particularly in awe of my white skin and odd-colored hair. They couldn't help themselves from always having to touch some part of me. All the time. While yelling "Mzungu!" because obviously, nobody else could see I was white!

By the end of our time there, I was paying one of the kids to do my laundry. Which can be described as taking my clothes down to the beach, dunking them in the water, and then hanging them in the trees to dry, and leaving me to find shorts and tanks and undies blowing around the campsite in the wind.

It wasn't until later, when we took one of the old boats out for a paddle, that we realized the next beach over was being used as the village toilet (back to that basic sanitation issue), and that it wasn't the best idea to be washing clothes or swimming in the lake. Because of that misjudgment, I returned stateside with an internal virus that was very common in Africa but had not been heard of in the US. After a few unsuccessful doctor visits, my sister, Cindy, who was a lab technician, called the Center for Disease Control in Atlanta, Georgia, to find out how to cure me! Turns out, the common name of Bilharzia in Africa was not known amongst the US doctors.

Showering at that particular hostel was also an experience unto itself. We had to schedule appointments. Said shower time had to be somewhere around late morning, after breakfast was served. This would give our host, Paul, time to collect the wood and make the fire under the metal water container – which I estimated held at least 30 gallons of water. Within an hour or two, the water would be hot enough to be scooped into three-gallon buckets, which then were hung on hooks, in their own stalls, in the shower house.

The shower participant (I use this word specifically because it was like being on some sort of reality TV show, which didn't exist back then!) would then enter their own stall, pull on their own private bucket handle that slowly tilted the bucket and let out a dribble of hot water that splashed right on top of their head. It was a very specific dance between timing and heat. But when all the specifics matched up, it was quite the exquisite experience! Let's just say that showering was a rare form of enjoyment while traveling in such a manner. Paul's shower system sure beat the hell out of jumping in the lake with a bar of soap.

And then there was Lake Malawi, measuring almost 360 miles long and about fifty miles wide at the widest part. It's huge – and impressive! It ranks up there, statistically as one of the biggest in the world, fourth largest by volume and ninth largest by surface area. It's a shame that during that time of my life I was just too busy getting drunk to really give it much thought or regard at all. Although, the local wildlife won my attention and respect after a few instances.

All the overlanders, as I'll call them, went swimming one afternoon. We found a lovely beach that had a floating dock we could swim to that was a respectable swim without too much effort. So, there we were, about six of us, sunning ourselves on our lovely little dock in the middle of our lovely little/big lake, and having a lovely time of it. One by one, each of us took our leave of the basking dock and jumped in to swim back to shore. Before I knew it, I was the sole sunbather left.

It was about this time I looked around and realized there was a hippo not too far out that just seemed to be swimming by. Really, I gave it very little notice. Until it started swimming directly for the dock. Now, we had all been given "the talk" about hippos and crocs in the water. Always keep an eye out, never be alone, always use the buddy system, blah, blah, blah. And, of course, we were all young, drunk, stoned, and mostly too preoccupied with having a good time to actually listen to – let alone take heed of – these warnings.

And now, there I was, all by myself, watching a hippo swim directly for me, the deadliest animal in Africa, responsible for killing approximately 500 people per year, and among the deadliest beasts in the world. They are highly aggressive and given their trails of carnage, seem to like killing things. I don't know how funny I looked that day, but I do know that I covered the distance between that dock and the shore in record time.

My adrenaline was pumping like a madman after an eight ball and I felt like one of those cartoon characters swimming so fast that I never even touched the water. I also know that I am here, writing this story, so I did make it to the shore before the hippo made it to me. Who knew such a huge, weighty beast could move so freaking fast, even in water (I mean, the hippo, not me)?! Note to self and readers – heed warnings when in hippo- and croc-infested waters.

My heart still ached from thoughts of Warren, but the hurt was becoming at least slightly more bearable. It was less frequent that sleep came through tears and waking came through sobs. Nighttime was still hard, but there were so many distractions to keep my mind and heart occupied that I was thankful. Especially while sleeping in a tent. Take fire ants, for instance….

I store my backpack in the vestibule of my tent at night in order to gain a few more inches of sleeping room. I'm not sure if it was fortuitous or not that one night an army of fire ants chose the back padding of my pack as a fine dining experience. There was nothing left but a big hole where my cushy padding should have been. Bummer for my pack, but a huge relief that the ants partook of my bag instead of my flesh.

African fire ants. Whoever came up with their name must have had a first-hand experience of their capabilities. Not only do they bite, but while they hold their prey captive with their pinchers, they inflict more torture with their back stinger. And they can sting multiple times. Weapons at the ready – at both ends. Double whammy! Ouch.

And then there was that night while camping with Pippa that a hyena mistook her hiking boot for a fine meal of animal hide. Luckily for her, it only tried to grab its prize from the outside of the tent and didn't see it necessary to rip it open first. Unluckily for the hyena, Pippa slept lightly and had a good mule kick! A hyena's jaws are definitely something you don't want to find one of your body parts between. So, yes, these scary incidents helped me not obsess over my broken heart and my bitterness towards Warren. But even the bite of a fire ant or the jaws of the hyena weren't sufficient to completely distract me. Although given the choice, the pain from the fire ant seemed the preferred alternative!

***

While traveling through various countries on the overland truck, naturally we had to cross borders. Sometimes this endeavor was quite a trial, with ten foreign travelers, along with our fearless, foreign, driving team, all on a foreign commercial truck. With every border crossing, it was more or less an each-to-their-own situation. Yes, we were a unit traveling together, but not really. As far as checking passports, we were all on our own.

The crossings from Zimbabwe to Zaire, and then again from Zaire to Malawi, were no big deal. Pim and Magot parked the truck, and we all had to disembark from the sanctuary of our canvas-enclosed truck bed. All of our individual belongings had to be unloaded and set at our feet as we lined up, awaiting our turn to be scrutinized by the border patrol guard. I was becoming accustomed to the questions:

"Where are you from? How long do you plan on staying? Where do you plan on going? Why are you here? Are you visiting anyone in this country?"

The one thing that I wasn't getting used to: machine guns. I couldn't help but notice that, no matter what country I visited in Africa, the police, members of the military, other powers in charge, loved to show off their armaments. Machine guns were proudly flaunted in plain view, the officers standing tall, all puffed up with the illusionary bravado that a highly polished, deadly weapon so easily seemed to encourage.

I will go out on a limb here and bring gender into the equation. Of course, this is my own point of view, and as I have become aware, not everyone shares my opinion (that's the understatement of the century!). Since I can't ever recall coming across a female police officer in Africa, I equated this proud show of munitions in direct correlation to testosterone levels. Boys and their toys. For the most part, I was usually very thankful that their testosterone levels seemed to be in check, and we rarely had any major issues getting from country to country. But to each rule there is an exception. And mine came at the Zambia/Tanzania border.

We prepared for the usual crossing. All of us had our stuff out and ready. Passports in hand. Answers prepared. Each one of us going through the motions as we were called to do. But they weren't happy with me at that particular border. The border guard didn't like my answers, and I was grabbed, not so gently, and thrust into a room in a concrete building nearby. This unhappy, machine-gun-wielding officer yelled something in his native tongue while pointing at one of the two chairs in the room. I obliged and abruptly sat. He then disappeared for a few very long and disconcerting minutes. The office was dark. There was one opening in the concrete, just above the chair opposite me, across from a big, metal desk topped with laminate.

As was typical in Africa, the hole was accepted as a window, but contained no glass or framing. Besides the chair I occupied, there was only one other chair. Both were plastic with metal legs, and dirty enough that I couldn't identify their original color. The laminate was peeling off the corners of the desk, and the room was coated in so much dirt and dust that I wasn't sure if the walls were actually painted black or if it was just the accumulation of decades of grime. I took all of this in subconsciously during my few brief minutes alone.

Then the guard burst through the door, with two more patrol officers in tow. I presumed they were officers given they all shouldered weaponry and wore the same extremely dirty, dark-blue uniforms and black, calf-high combat boots. Now I was really beginning to sweat. In sharp contrast to their skin the color of coal, their eyes and teeth were the only lightness I could see clearly gleaming in the dark dinginess of the concrete room. And all I knew in that moment was that my white privilege was an anchor that had the power to drown me.

"Oh shit, this is bad," my brain repeated nervously, over and over again.

One of the officers took a seat opposite me behind the desk. Another half leaned on the side of the desk with the peeling laminate, while the other stood guard in front of the closed door. They were very interested in my American citizenship, asking all kinds of questions about where I was from, and what I did for work back home. No voices were raised. It was all kept very quiet and low key. But the tension and my fear were palpable. I was doing everything I could to keep it together. Just answer their questions as best I was able while trying to figure out what they wanted from me.

Was it sex? Was I about to be raped? My fear overrode my intuition. I couldn't pinpoint what the hell was going on. I was so confused and terrified. The questions just kept coming, and my stammering answers were becoming jumbled and chaotic. Suddenly, it clicked. It was money. They wanted money.

Being an American is rarely a bonus while traveling abroad. In this case, it was almost my undoing. I was adamant in my explanations that I had no money; I was just a broke backpacker hitchhiking around their continent. Really, I was…. The few bills and coins I had were laid out on the table along with my passport. I showed them my empty wallet. The questions didn't stop. They didn't believe me.

"You are American. If you don't have money here, you can get it. It will cost you to go across our border. You must pay," and on and on they went, in their broken English.

Abruptly, the guy doing the questioning stood up and slightly leaned across the desk. It was so abrupt that it took me a minute to comprehend.
There was a gun at my head.
The shit just got real. Quick. I froze. My whole body went on pause. Not a blink. Not a breath. My brain shut down. I believe my heart even stopped beating. Everything just stopped. It wasn't a machine gun, but a smaller weapon that was pulled from a holster on his hip. All I remember, in that moment, was looking into that black man's very white eyes.

"Please. Please. Please. Don't hurt me," my eyes begged, while my throat went immediately dry and rendered me incapable of speaking.

It only took a moment. A moment that felt like the timelessness of a black hole. I don't know if he was bluffing or not, but believe me, if I had had anything to give him, it would have all been his in that instant. He slowly took the barrel of the gun off my temple and re-holstered it on his hip. And that was that. My passport was stamped, the door was opened, and my inquisitors were wishing me happy travels, all flashy white teeth, eyes, and guns.

I have no idea how I removed myself from that concrete block and back into the truck. My legs were shaking, I was sweating profusely from every pore in my body, tears were streaming down my cheeks, and I had an immense urge to throw up. Everyone on the truck was all packed up and waiting for me and full of questions that I had no voice to answer.

It took a while for me to pull myself together again. But my state of shock was so strong that I don't believe I ever relayed that scene to anyone. It was too intense to relive and the emotional memories got shoved way down somewhere in the recesses of my soul. Out of my sheer terror and absolute silence soon came an intense happiness to be alive, and within a few hours, I was stupidly joyful. All I could do was smile for the hours before we set up camp and retired for the night. I was so fucking glad to be alive!

In retrospect, I'm sure they were just screwing with me. Logic says there is no way some African border patrol officer could get away with shooting an American tourist. But when there was a gun resting against my temple, there was no logic streaming through my mind. None. And, of course, there was the fact that nobody knew where I was. Usually not even me! The people I was traveling with on the truck had no way of getting in touch with anyone in my life. But that's part of traveling, I guess. I signed up for this. I had definitely gotten myself in way further than I had bargained for on this African excursion, but there was no stopping me. Not even a gun to the head. I was immersed, and I was staying that way.

The ironic fact about that border crossing event was that I did not, in fact, have any money. Back in those days, money for traveling was either as travelers' checks, or on a Visa that I could draw cash from at a bank. By that point, I had cashed in all of my travelers' checks, and only had the small bit left that I had thrown out on the table in that horrid concrete room. Not nearly enough to appease the soldiers who were interrogating me. I had been trying to call either Lynn or Mom to get some money so I could keep on traveling. My sister was my first choice given that my mother was going to need a lot more explaining, but by that point I wasn't picky! Once again, I was only somewhat aware of my absolute privilege at the time – spoiled white girl that I was.

Finding a telephone while traipsing around Africa in an overland truck is not easy. While going through Tanzania, we stopped in a little village to camp. I was told there was a public phone available in the next town over, at the post office, which was only open a few hours a day. So, I went in search of that beloved chance to get some money sent my way. The post office was almost ten kilometers distant, a little more than six miles, and I had no choice but to walk.

Off I went, into the dusty, sun-beaten African bush, towards a promised but unknown telephone. Fortunately for me, I made it to the next town, and found the post office, which, in fact, had a telephone available for public use (for a fee, of course). Unfortunately for me, there were about twenty people in line already and the post office was only open for a few hours. Hot and tired, trying not to be discouraged, I waited. And then the post office closed before my turn came.

Down the road I went again, headed for the campsite, only to turn around and return, another ten kilometers, back to the post office the next morning. This time, I got my chance. Which, by "my chance" literally meant three minutes of connection time for my phone call. The Gods were smiling on me that day, because, after multiple times of calls with no answer, this time my mom picked up. Ohhhhhh, she was so beyond furious!!

"Where are you?! Where have you been?! I've been going out of my mind with worry!" to which I had to cut her off mid-sentence in order to plead for money before my three-minute time was up and I had to go to the back of the line again. Attempting to explain my situation to my crazy anxious mother, and persuading her to send money to my Visa account, all in under three minutes seemed just about as likely as a sloth scaling Mt. Everest! Somehow, I made it happen, and was able to relay my account number across the line so she could drop me enough money to get back to South Africa to catch my flight back home.

Only I left out a crucial piece of information, which I will blame on the brief amount of time I had to explain. I had no plan of heading back to South Africa soon. Okay, so I was a completely shitty daughter and all-around horrible human being that day, completely self-absorbed and focused on my selfish needs. But… Well, that's about it. I have no excuse for my utter narcissistic actions. Besides the fact that I was having an otherworldly experience and had no desire for it to end!

I did not turn around and head for a plane in South Africa, as I had implied. Mom came through for me, and I was able to continue along my merry, oblivious, ego-centric travels. In fact, it would be another two months before my poor mother would hear from me once more. I would be reminded of that little omission for the rest of my adult life.

***

As I touched on briefly, while witnessing the ocean baptism in Africa, my feelings towards organized religion are not warm and fuzzy. I'm not a believer, and don't think of myself as needing to be born again. As the saying goes, I was born just fine the first time, thank you. I have no problem with Jesus, but his followers leave a lot to be desired.

You can imagine my absolute amazement and disbelief when, one of those days hanging off the side of our trusty overland vehicle, the truck happened to pass by a Jehovah's Witness sign. Huh? What?! We were in the middle of the
African bush. I mean, this wasn't like rural Pennsylvania or something. The AFRICAN BUSH, for God's sake! What the actual fuck???

I guess I shouldn't have been so surprised. I mean, missionaries have been trying to "tame the wild indigenous tribes" for thousands of years. But to actually witness it in such a remote and far-reaching location was beyond my comprehension. My emotions started with shock, then moved quickly towards anger. Don't get me wrong, I'm not specifically into telling people what they can and can't believe. I think there's even a church out there called the Church of the Flying Spaghetti Monster. Good for them. Pray to that pasta. Whatever makes you happy. My motto is, go ahead and believe whatever you want, under two conditions: it doesn't hurt anyone or anything, and you don't try to shove it down my throat.

One of the main priorities of the Jehovah's Witness church is to convert as many people as its members can.

The more people you convert, the faster track you are on for a glorious encounter with God, or some such thing. So, this really pisses me off. Knowing that these devout followers are out there somewhere in the bush trying to convert all the local tribespeople to the "chosen path."

For God's sake (pun intended), leave them alone! They really have a lot more figured out than we do. They don't need an upgrade to a new and improved, super-sized religion. They don't need to be saved. The whole idea is just ludicrous. Why can't we, as humans, just honor other humans and their beliefs? Why can't we respect other ways of being? Why can't all of our Gods just get together and decide to actually love and accept everyone?

Oh, wait, it's not the Gods, it's the people. We just can't seem to walk our talk, I guess. Ugh… How religion has ruled the world forever and ever is totally beyond my understanding. It just seems so obvious to me that the entire basis of organized religion is to keep people in fear. Wasn't Jesus supposed to be the epitome of love, compassion, acceptance, and understanding? How did our modern version of religion stray so far from that truth? Modern Christians rarely walk that talk, from what I have experienced.

Of all the ironies: a homophobic old man, dressed in robes and a pointy hat, all decked out with shiny adornments, surrounded in an ornate castle with other similarly robed homophobic old men, running the world... Well, it's pretty self-explanatory. And now you know how I feel about organized religion.

***

> *"When you play the flute in Zanzibar, all Africa dances." –*
> *Zanzibar proverb*

At the junction to Dar es Salaam, which is on the coast of Tanzania, Derek, Pippa, and I, plus two others from the overland truck, Claire and Ben, took leave of our fearless leaders, Pim and Margo, and the rest of our fellow travelers who were continuing their journey north. After a few weeks on the truck, we had concluded it was time for us to branch out. See the sights face-to-face instead of wheeling past from the safety of our government-issued armored vehicle. We jumped off, said our goodbyes, and took our places along the side of the road to wait for the local bus that would take us to the coast of the Indian Ocean.

We made quite the sight, the five of us all caked in dirt and sweat, our backpacks overflowing, as we waited expectantly for our first local bus ride. When the bus arrived, it was customary for the locals to throw their bags and belongings onto the top while they clambered aboard with whatever they were dragging along. Babies, goods for sale, chickens, goats, pigs… You name it; it went on the bus. But none of us trusted our backpacks to be out of our sight. We had been warned that separation from them could be permanent. When the bus was full, local men started riding on the top with all the bags. I don't want to cast aspersions or fuel potentially mistaken assumptions. But those riding shotgun were reputed to think of themselves as self-appointed baggage inspectors who felt free to confiscate whatever they believed another passenger should not have.

So, we became one with our packs loaded with our earthly goods and off we went, into the cramped chaos, following each other like sheep to the slaughter. As far as we could see, we were the only whites in the vicinity, and it seemed our presence was a novel surprise for most of the locals. Because we were all smashed into our seats with our huge packs taking up whatever breathing space we had in front of us, there was little chance of having a pig or chicken or child shoved on our laps. Later we learned it was not unusual for locals to do such things; they rather relished inflicting more discomfort on the unwitting traveler.

Travel time to Dar es Salaam was to be about two hours, during which Pippa and I, who were seated right next to one another, found great delight in our immersion into local transportation. It was hotter than an inferno at the back of that bus, and we were sweating our asses off underneath all of our belongings, packed like sardines in a can. Yet we were having the time of our lives. Loving every second of our discomfort. Dizzy with excitement of the unknown. At every stop, locals would try to sell us all sorts of items through the bus windows, most of which we turned down.

But we did partake of some boiled eggs sold by a tall, skinny, black-as-night woman with bright, white teething gleaming like the sun on fresh winter snow. She was all smiles. We were all smiles. Not that the flavor was anything extraordinary, but I believe they were the best eggs either of us had ever eaten – bought from the window of our local bus. For me, they were the most memorable. We savored every morsel, sweat dripping from our brows.

When we finally arrived at Dar es Salaam (which is a complete shithole, by the way) we were turned down for lodging at the first place we went to. And then the second, as well. It seemed that finding accommodation for five of us, on short notice, was not to happen. Our high spirits began to wane. We were trying to keep up our hopes of finding somewhere to stay in the utter craziness of this disgusting, overpopulated city.

Luckily, we accepted a proposition from some local men to help find us tickets to Zanzibar, the exotic and tantalizing "Spice Island(s)" of Africa, which is where we were heading anyway. (Zanzibar is actually an archipelago of islands, whose history goes back 20,000 years.) Within an hour, we found ourselves happily situated on a ferry headed for our island destination, some 22 miles from the coast. It was a blessing in disguise that things didn't work out for us in Dar es Salaam because we were all besotted with Zanzibar within minutes of the ferry's landing.

After taking inventory, Ben and Claire found that one of their bags had been stolen somewhere along the way. The bag held only food and a pullover of Claire's, so the loss was far from monumental, though Claire was none too pleased. We exhaled a collective sigh of relief once on the streets of this Muslim island off the coast of Tanzania. It was no less chaotic, but it was much friendlier and cleaner. Outdoor vendors, who were lined up and down every street in sight, were happy and smiling. The people all seemed to have a much more uplifting life energy than in Dar es Salaam.

It had been a seemingly endless day of travel; we were thankful to soon find a comfortable, cheap sanctuary to call home for the time being, right in the middle of

Stone Town, the main square. We all thought Stone Town was cool because of its labyrinth of alleyways, its aromas and sounds, its ancient architecture, and particularly its massive wooden carved doors that were so beautiful and, at the same time, intimidating.

We later learned Stone Town is a very big deal. In 2000 it was named a United Nations World Heritage site. It's considered an outstanding example of the Swahili trading towns of East Africa, and people have lived there for 20,000 years. Its culture reflects the union of disparate elements of Africa, the Arab region, India, and Europe while retaining its indigenous elements. Within its confines is an area steeped in history that is now an urban cultural center distinct to the region.

And then there are the people. Mohammed, which seemed to be every man's name in those parts, was the hotel owner, Mohammed's, son. He was close to our age and took us in as his own, taking it upon himself to teach us basic Swahili daily. Enchanted by this island paradise, we were hungry to learn. Zanzibar really did seem to suit us.

It is indeed a magical place, a deeply spiritual place. It's almost entirely Muslim throughout the Archipelago.

I never knew what the Muslim faith entailed before. Now, I was to receive a world-class education. Another immersion experience. The bells of the mosque rang five times every day, at which time everyone would cease whatever they were doing, wherever they were, and kneel on the floor/ground for their prostrations. After a few days, we figured out the timing of the five daily prayers. The first was sometime around 5:00 am, second was precisely at noon, third was mid-afternoon, fourth was at six, and finally, the last call to prayer was around 8:00 pm. Each of these times, the mosque bells would ring and the world would come to a halt.

For just a few minutes, everyone joined in unison for their worship. We were told Allah commands that the devout prostrate on seven bones: forehead, palms, knees, and feet. Worshippers face the east towards Mecca and touch their foreheads to the ground a total of thirty-four or more times over the course of five calls to prayer. As non-Muslim foreigners, we were not required to pray and prostrate. But it was expected of us to stop and be still during prayer. We found it an essential demonstration of respect for our Muslim brothers and sisters and their way of life.

It was quite an unforgettable process to witness, because during prayer, time stood still. If we were haggling with a vendor over the price of some hand-carved item, or piece of clothing, the bartering stopped immediately, the vendor would hit the ground, do his prayers and prostrations, and then stand up to re-engage in our negotiations exactly where we had left off. And we, as witnesses, merely had to stand and wait for a few minutes until the prayers were finished.

Now, let's say we were standing at a newspaper kiosk in downtown Chicago, and suddenly the vendor just checked out for a couple of minutes. I would expect a lot of burgling during that small space of time. But no, not here. Prayer times were like a truce zone. If even the thought of something like burglary crossed someone's mind during prayer times, I'm more than sure Allah's wrath would strike him or her down instantly. Nope. Crime just didn't happen during prayers.

***

"Silverback" lovingly became Derek's nickname. At the ripe old age of twenty-six, his hair was beginning to turn gray; Pippa and I were not taking the blame. In no way would
Derek be considered a small guy, and his plan on leaving Pippa and me so he could go hang with some gorillas in Zaire (which changed back to Congo in 1997), all combined to make it a fitting term of endearment.

Our Silverback was the best travel companion a girl could ask for. While his calm disposition would never allow him to raise a finger to anyone, his sheer size was a natural deterrent for pickpockets or other evildoers and made us feel safe when wandering through even the sketchiest of sketchy areas. Someone would have to be pretty ballsy to take on our Silverback! Contrary to his menacing magnitude, Derek was really just a big softy.

On one of our first nights in the Stone Town hotel, the three of us were getting situated for bed in our cozy, shared room, desperately trying to untangle the cheap, yet absolutely necessary, mess of white mesh hanging above each of our single platform mattresses. It was not an option to forego mosquito netting in these parts, for fear of the highly menacing little vampires that swarmed us continually throughout both night and day.

The nights seemed to be their favorite time for blood sucking. And suck blood they did, by the gallons, it seemed! Of course, the netting helped little in the way of airflow, but such were our dilemmas. Be eaten alive, slowly and maddeningly, or become overwhelmed by the oppression of heat and humidity.

The meager diversion of air from what they considered ceiling fans wasn't much help with the mosquito nets covering us. Especially Derek's. After multiple attempts and much profanity, he succumbed to a burrito-like mesh wrapping for the night. He was too tall for the netting to fit from his head to his toes while remaining in a hanging position. So, he simply wrapped it around him like a blanket and gave up the fight, while enduring the onslaught of laughter from both Pippa and me. Funny as he looked, I have no idea how he slept like that. Poor guy!

Being a tourist in Zanzibar, although quite magical, had some cultural drawbacks. Outdoor vendors in Stone Town were crammed into side streets and alleys, along with hundreds of Muslim locals trying to get from here to there.

The British couple that joined us from the overland truck, Ben and Claire, were still with us at that juncture.

Claire was a small, petite blond with blue eyes; she was having a hard time with the whole traveling scene. She'd had a few things stolen along her travels so far and wasn't thinking highly of African people in general by that point. After hanging out with them both for a while, we all started to understand that this just might not be her thing. Being around Muslim people, especially as white women, both Pippa and I adapted our fashion style. Basically, be respectful.

Typically, Muslim women were well-covered in thin, flowy robes and scarves, including their hair. It wasn't super extreme, like burkas, but it was their custom to cover themselves. So, we made sure that we didn't wear tank tops or shorts and, considering the heat, it was a big deal. However, sarongs were light and airy, and covered enough of our whiteness that we seemed not to offend too much. But Claire just didn't get it. She complained she was too hot and wore tank tops and short shorts into the local streets and markets.

The closeness of the comings and goings in Stone Town made bodily contact inevitable, and we were all regularly bumping into people and brushing up against the oncoming flow of humanity in the over-crowded streets. It was obvious to Pippa and me that the local Muslim women did not approve of Claire's choice of clothing. During one of our outings, she got a good, hard, somewhat painful pinch, followed by a punch in the arm from a group of passing Muslim women. Hard enough that it bruised her upper arm.

It all happened quickly and at close proximity, so we couldn't identify the culprit, but the event left Claire highly upset. She felt victimized. The rest of us couldn't help but find her at fault, though we said nothing. She just didn't seem to understand the meaning of respectful travel. Or to even care. Between her unwillingness to respect Muslim traditions regarding feminine propriety, flaunting her personal belongings in public, and then wondering why she was robbed, we weren't at all surprised when Ben and Claire announced their departure from Zanzibar, and soon after that, their departure from Africa altogether.

While they were still with us, the five of us – Pippa, Derek, Ben, Claire, and I decided to rent little street motorbikes, called Vespas, to visit the beaches on the other side of the island. We got three Vespas in total. One for Ben and Claire to share, one for Derek to share, and one for either Pippa or me to take on our own.

Our adventure started on the city roads of town, winding our way through the crazed scene of vendors, cars/motorcycles/trucks/taxis, pedestrians, and animals, none of which had a specific lane or flow of direction. Just a hodgepodge of manic chaos that was excessively stressful. Death and destruction constantly reared their ugly heads and then dissipated just as quickly.

The relief of reaching the dirt roads on the outskirts of town disappeared instantly when we realized they were full of potholes and ruts, and the cows that had free range over the island liked to hang out in the open areas of the roadways. We were in a real-time video game that could have been named "Driving Insanity."

Finally, we neared our destination, and the discomfort of the journey there vanished. As with so many other times during this trip, it was like stepping into a postcard. Sun shining in the clear blue sky above, winds rustling through the grassy branches of the palm trees that lined the white sand beach, translucent waters of the sea beckoning us. Completely iconic, unbelievable magnificence! We were all in our happy place and spent the afternoon swimming in the warm, clear salt water and chatting, or trying to chat as much as we could in a foreign language, with the local fishermen.

The dhow is the traditional wooden boat they use. It's a smaller rig, maybe about fifteen to twenty-five feet long or so, and has a single mast with a slanted, triangular sail. They originated in the area of the Red Sea for transporting goods, such as slaves, fruit, fresh water, and spices, and, as we witnessed firsthand, they were used for fishing and tourist transport in Zanzibar. Their tilted single sails propelled by the warm ocean winds across the azure waters of this island paradise were eye-candy to us adventuring tourists. This was the stuff of our dreams!

After we had all become sufficiently sunburnt and thoroughly covered in sand, we jumped back on our trusty little Vespas and headed to our Stone Town home. Derek and Pippa were on one, Ben and Claire had the other, while I was flying solo on the last of three.

Unfortunately, as I believe it to have happened, one of my tires got caught in a dried mud rut and pulled my little motorbike right off the road. Ending up sideways in the bushes off the side of the road filled me with all kinds of anxiety and I couldn't make myself get back into the driver's seat after that.

As in so many other times in our travels, Derek came to the rescue, and I was once again indebted to him. He took control of my mischievous bike, piloted it back to the hotel and, later, to the rental shop. While Pippa was given her opportunity to make me look like an idiot driver. She seemed to have no problem getting her Vespa back in one piece.

Okay, so what else must you do when you are in the famed Spice Islands of Africa? Take a Spice Tour, of course. And this spice tour blew the mind of this woman who would later become a chef and restaurant owner (though I didn't know these things at the time).

Zanzibar's spice heritage harkens back more than 400 years. Our tour brought us to an old plantation which, after the slave trade was abolished, was turned into a farm that grew hundreds of spices and fruits as a tourist attraction. Not that we were much into tourist attractions, but this place was absolutely amazing!

The farm itself was the best surprise. I had expected orderly rows of trees and shrubs. Instead, it resembled a huge, overgrown jungle of fruits and spices growing hodgepodge throughout the property. It was disorderly and wild and wonderful, and home to hundreds of incredible and exotic fruits and spices none of us had ever had the chance to experience firsthand.

Nutmeg encased in its web of brilliant red mace, cinnamon curls shaved from the inside of the tree bark, big fat bean pods picked right from the tree and scraped to extract vanilla seeds, fruit shaped like stars cut into beautiful slices for us to enjoy, cassava and ginger root pulled right out of the ground, three types and colors of peppercorn shaken from their pods, the red dye from the achiote seeds, lemongrass and coconut, and, of course, spices of all kinds.

The shining star of their spices being the clove, the spice that Zanzibar was known for during the previous era of slavery. Amazingly, the clove is a dried flower bud of a big tree. Before it's harvested and dried, when it looks like a little dark brown star-headed pushpin for your roasted pig, it's actually a bunch of beautiful flowers that haven't come into bud yet. The cloves are a muted shade of light green when picked, and when let go to flower will become a soft shade of red.

Little was said about the stories behind the slave trade and the growing and harvesting of cloves in the 1800's. As with slavery anywhere, the tales were horrid.

The tour ended in a tiny, open-air, thatched-roof hut where Pippa and I were delighted to experience local henna artistry on our palms. Our trusty Silverback peered over our shoulders, fascinated by the artists and the process. I think he wanted tattoos, also.

The memories of that day, of the intoxicating fragrances and tastes of the fruits and spices we sampled, are with me decades later. I have shared many stories about that tour and the things I've learned about exotic foods and flavors in my commercial kitchens and cooking classes. I trust I will continue to put those lessons to good use. What a difference a day can make in the rich tapestry of one's life.

***

Our time with Derek had come to an end. Both Pippa and I did everything we could to talk him into staying with us, and remain the Three Stooges, but previous to meeting us he had made plans to go to the jungles of Zaire to see the glorious primates we all know as gorillas. (Between 1971 and 1997 it was known as Zaire. After that, it changed to the DRC – the Democratic Republic of the Congo. Long story… All very political. But for us, it was Zaire.) The Silverback was going to meet his kin (sadly, these gorillas are currently, in 2023, on the critically endangered list). Wistfully, we said our goodbyes and bade well wishes, hoping that our paths would cross again sometime soon. And, thus, the adventures of Pippa and Lisa began.

What would we have done without our trusty deck of playing cards? Thankfully, I never had to ask that question. Rummy was the name of the game and, in normal settings, the total score would have gone to 500 points. But backpacking through Africa was no normal setting, and the epic Rummy game that we began lasted for over a month. A month of hitchhiking, mountain adventures, an African safari, and endless hostel stays. We just broke out the deck of cards whenever we felt idle and needed something to do. Nobody else was ever invited to join the game, but there were more than a few times when it became a spectator sport for other travelers looking to fill a few minutes.

Our scorecard surpassed the 500-point mark early on in our travels, and just kept ranging higher and loftier. Playing one long, suspense-filled, never-ending game just seemed more enticing – and fun – than one game after another. I'm still not sure, to this day, who actually was the victor. Somewhere in that month of continuous playing, the entire idea of an overall winner was abandoned. But I do remember many, many hours spent shuffling, dealing, plotting, winning, and losing. Sometimes it was by the light of the torch in the tent; a few nights were by firelight beneath the protection of a rock ledge, and other similarly outlandish settings. That was one unforgettably epic game of cards!!

Pippa and I quickly learned that hitchhiking was a much easier, and usually cheaper, option than public transportation. Although, we also found out that most drivers did expect some form of payment for offering a ride, even if it was just a small token. It took us a few "free" rides to figure this one out, after being surprised when asked for money upon arrival at our destination.

But we were more than happy to accommodate, since it was always significantly less than our other alternatives, and it was invariably faster than waiting for a local bus. Hitching rides became an adventure in and of itself. Two white, English speaking, usually dust-covered and unshowered, backpack toting, young women were not a common sight on the side of the road in rural Africa.

So, there we were, Pippa and I, about to jump into the back of a small, dusty, beat-up pickup truck which already contained about a dozen or so locals. (We were really loving the visual of deep mocha faces with shiny white eyes and teeth greeting us as we plodded across the continent.) Riding in open vehicles was becoming one perpetual adventure! More than not, the locals were very welcoming to us in their environment. Even despite how utterly shitty most whites in their history had treated them.

Our hitchhiking excursion of the day had started out, as usual, on the side of a not-so-often traveled dirt road – not unlike most roads in rural Africa – with our thumbs out, hoping for a decent, quick, and cheap ride. Decent, meaning not getting abducted or sold into the sex trade; quick meaning getting a ride sometime within two hours from when we started out; and cheap, meaning not having to pay more than a few dollars for any given ride, although it was usually a few cents.

As we clambered over the sides of the pickup bed, a few of the locals scurried out of the way to make room for us, and we happily and thankfully took the open spots available. Within mere moments of sniffing the air, puzzled, we discovered that we were, in fact, sitting on sacks of dead fish. They were little dead fish, which made for a more comfortable seat than big dead fish, but little or big, dead fish all have the same stench. WHEW!!! The locals didn't seem to mind one bit, and Pippa and I were able to find humor in our situation and smiled and laughed through the entire ride.

Luckily, it was only a few miles before we were dropped at our destination, and the driver didn't charge us a cent for the ride, which was very kind of him. He could have made us pay for the privilege of sitting on dead fish and subsequently wreaking of carnage. He didn't take the opportunity to rip off the white daughters of imperialism. Even after changing our clothes, especially our shorts, we were fortunate enough that we had access to hot showers at the hostel to help sink the stink. The clothes had to be stored in plastic bags in our backpacks for a few more days to get the same reprieve. Oh, the things we did to fit into our surroundings!

A huge endeavor of ours was to hike in the Chimanimani Mountains of Zimbabwe. Somewhere along the way, we had heard about this unbelievably beautiful hike and put it on our bucket list. We got ourselves ready for a few days in the mountains – sleeping bags, clothing for both cool nights and hot days, food for about two days for both of us, and, of course, the playing cards. We hitched a ride to the trailhead and started our hike.

    Neither Pippa nor I were self-aware enough to realize that we had both gained some weight while traveling and were not quite fit and trim enough for a two-day hike up some pretty strenuously steep trails with packs on our backs. After about five hours of sweating profusely and copious amounts of profanity, we discovered we were not on the right trail to the caves where we planned to spend the night. We bumped into a few other hikers who pointed us to a rangers' cabin that might afford us shelter. Then we could head out in the morning in search of the caves again.

    As dusk was descending, we found the cabin, which indeed did have two empty beds for our lost asses. Exhausted, we hunkered down to make dinner for the evening. Unfortunately for us, the can of corn that we dumped on our rice mixture was rancid, ruining our entire meal. After hiking in scorching heat for hours that day, we were practically in tears over this culinary debacle. The other hikers sharing the cabin took pity on us and gifted us a can of their soup to share. Ahhhhhh, the beauty of finding "family" in the wild. Such gratitude for their abundant offering!

The next morning found us on the trail again, this time pointed in the direction of the caves we wanted to find so badly. True to their word, as the other hikers had told us, the caves, which were actually just rocky overhangs, were no more than a two-hour hike from the rangers' cabin. And there was nobody in sight. They were all ours and we were overjoyed.

That afternoon, we lounged in the warm, sunny fields by our little overhangs. As evening came, we set up our sleeping bags and made a fire to not only warm ourselves, but also to light up our ongoing game of Rummy. Dinner was yet another somewhat crappy, yet edible, culinary surprise out of a can. But really, anything is a wondrously delicious meal when enjoyed by a campfire under a rock overhang after a few hours' hike. After our meal and card game, we settled in for what we hoped was going to be a deep and enjoyable sleep, at least as good as we could hope for while sleeping on the ground in our sleeping bags in an open cave-like situation.

Enter the mice. I don't mind mice, as in, they don't freak me out or anything. But that night, the mice found it highly enjoyable to run across our sleeping bags and over our faces.
Over and over and over again. I learned that Pippa was not a big fan of mice, especially when they were climbing on her face while she was sleeping. It did not make for a

deep and enjoyable sleep. We slept in for a while after the sun came up and the mice had gone away. We shared a breakfast of avocado on bread and decided that we didn't want to leave.

With our mishap the first night of not finding the caves and staying at the rangers' cabin, and the rancid can of corn that ruined dinner, we started out low on our two days food supply, but we decided we were willing to live on one large African avocado for another night's stay. African avocados are at least double the size of the ones we're used to in the States that actually come from Mexico. Both of us were highly aware of our extra storage of body fat over the past few weeks and figured it would probably do us good, a bit of fasting.

Pippa donned her day pack and decided to hike the short distance to the Mozambique border to put foot in yet another African country, but I wasn't feeling it and chose to stick around our little cave dwelling for the afternoon and be sloth-like. Off she went, while I undertook the strenuous task of basking in the sun. It wasn't long before the sky clouded over and rudely interrupted my sunbathing, but when I looked up, I realized it wasn't clouds.

A slight haze had filled the sky and the smell of smoke overtook my nostrils. It had started snowing grey instead of white flakes. There was a wildfire coming up over the ridge not far from our cozy rock ledge campsite!

Lisa Ruoff

I had just a few minutes to run around collecting what I took to be our most prized possessions and head for the stream not far from camp.

Scrambling onto the protection of a rock surrounded by water, I watched in terrified amazement as the wildfire ate up the dry grasses and burnt its way destructively from the hillside and through the fields beyond our little campsite. Pippa somehow missed the whole sordid scene while on her hike to Mozambique and came back to find a scorched landscape. Luckily for us, there really wasn't much in the way of food for the fire, and it moved through quickly, without too much destruction. We were able to stay in our little enclave without a significant charcoal mess to worry about. Although it made for quite a difficult time finding firewood for the evening!

Quite the sight we must have been, two happy campers, huddled under our rock ledge, surrounded by black ashes swirling about in the breeze, with only an avocado to share for sustenance. The Chimanimani mountains were incredibly beautiful though, and we found our predicament quite amusing. We fell asleep laughing at ourselves under a starry sky. The Universe definitely had a sense of humor and we weren't going to let our minor mishap get us down!

Our avocado was enough to get us through until we finally made our way back down the mountains, in the pouring rain, and into the closest town. My prize was a steaming hot French press coffee at a local café after a week of no caffeine, and I relished every second of it!

* * *

In all the hiking exploits that Pippa and I had, there were a few that yielded thought-provoking life lessons. I can't necessarily speak for Pippa, but growing up as a somewhat spoiled, very white, upper-middle-class, American female definitely shaped my personal outlook on my travels through a third-world country. My perspective of the world was through my own rose-colored glasses, and the reality of it was that I was completely unaware of how the rest of the world lived.

For instance, when I shared my upcoming adventures to Africa with friends and family, it was not unusual for people to worry about my safety. Actually, I probably should have been way more concerned than I was! But sometimes the naïveté of youth is actually a blessing in disguise. As far as I knew, I was invincible. There was nothing to fear.

Yes, Africa had its fair share of crime and disease, but, of course, I would be untouched by any of that. How could that possibly harm me? I was an American, right?!

Or so I was raised to believe… As I'm writing this, at the ripe old age of fifty-one, I obviously lived to tell all the stories, but they didn't come without their close calls or lessons.

I experienced an ego-shattering epiphany while hiking through yet some more beautifully majestic remote mountains. As if there could even be more beautiful, majestic mountains. But this was Africa. And as John Hemingway wrote, "If I have ever seen magic, it is in
Africa."

Once again, Pippa and I found ourselves hiking off the beaten path and through some isolated rural villages. It was not unusual for local children to come running straight for us as soon as we were in sight. We learned they were just unabashedly curious about our white skin and funny hair. Soon we came to relish our brief encounters with these local kids. They were always full of laughter, joy, and unrelenting conversation, usually in a foreign tongue not understood by our English ears. And they loved to get as close as possible; they had to touch us in one way or another. Usually, a child would hold onto each finger. More trailed behind trying to somehow be in contact with our skin or hair. That was the usual scenario, and how we emerged without broken fingers still astounds me.

On one of these occasions, I looked down and realized that my hiking boot had skinned the back of a little girl's bare heel and it was bleeding into the dirt. Immediately, I stopped and shooed the other kids away so I could try to make up for my clumsy stepping. After kneeling down on the dirt path to check out her small, but not insignificant contusion, I realized that I really had no way of making it better. The only solace I could offer was a crumpled-up tissue from my pocket, which I pressed onto her weeping heel. Although, as we found with most African children, she acted as if nothing at all had happened and she couldn't care the slightest that she was bleeding and possibly feeling some pain.

I felt absolutely horrid about the consequences of my clumsiness. Here these kids are, all running around with no shoes on, believing they are in need of nothing, and then my over-encumbered, clunky-footed, clueless, tourist self comes along and trods on a naked foot. Ugh. It didn't occur to me until I had a sufficient amount of this child's blood smeared on my hands that I might need to worry about some communicable disease.

This thought hit me like a ton of bricks, considering that it was the 1990s and AIDS was quite a valid concern at that time. What made me feel even worse was that I even had the thought that this little girl could possibly harm me. I was the intruder here. I was the one who made her bleed. I was the one at fault. Jesus, and my entitled, spoiled, first-world brain had to make me the victim. And the audacity of it is that most Americans wouldn't even understand what I'm talking about. I, and we, have been taught to fear everything outside of our safety bubble. And I had gladly taken a step out of that bubble for a reason. Because it made me sick. My entire being didn't want to believe that I was better than anyone else.

In that instant of looking at this little girl's blood on my hands, blood that was there because of my negligence, I got it. I completely understood the equality and oneness of us all. She was me and I was her, and I was willing to take on whatever that meant. I needed to step out of the fear that was so ingrained in me – ingrained in us all. Stop playing victim to every circumstance that could happen. I had to look the possibility of AIDS right in the face and tell it to fuck off, for so many reasons. Mostly for making me feel separate from and fearful of this beautiful little African child who stood smiling and joyful, and bleeding, in front of me.

Fuck AIDS, and fuck separateness. I chose to feel unity with her. And ya know what? I didn't get AIDS. Since that day, I have had many more opportunities to feel separate and fearful of people and situations. But I refuse. I refuse to let fear and a sense of being separate rule my life, I seek to embrace the unity and oneness of everything. When I'm really lucky, I can actually feel, taste, and believe it. That oneness is tangible. But I'm still a work in progress.

Another such instance of immediately being right-sized in the face of my own self-importance occurred again, while hiking in the mountains of that beautiful continent. What is it about the mountains in Africa? Are they a metaphor for trying to reach our highest, best selves? Could that be why I was having these humbling experiences and life-transforming revelations?

Pippa and I couldn't help but be reminded of our tremendous, good fortune and privilege as we walked through the remote mountain villages in our path. The children had touched our hearts, and we found ourselves wanting somehow to help them in whatever way we could. So, I decided to go to the source and ask what they needed most. More times than not, the answer was school supplies.

Our method of travel didn't lend itself to hauling books or notepads with us, but we decided upon one item that wouldn't weigh us down too much that could be a big help – pencils. Lo and behold, we were given a perfect opportunity – or so I thought – not long after we conceived our wonderful idea. On yet another hike through the mountains, we came across yet another rural village where the children all came running out to greet the mzungus walking by.

"How fantastic! Let's implement our 'giving plan' and spread love and joy to all!" or some such philanthropic thought, was the feeling of that moment.

As we handed out pencil after pencil to unbelieving, thankful, little grabbing hands, I felt so fulfilled. It was like I finally found some way of giving back and I was just as thankful as those children were to receive their gifts. There were shrill giggles and joyous laughter while they held up their highly coveted gifts of yellow #2 pencils. The children danced and shuffled in the dirt, and we were all encircled in a cloud of gritty happiness. All was well in the world. And then… We ran out of pencils. And there were still kids who hadn't received one.

To our amazement and horror, the kids who did not receive pencils promptly started beating on the kids who had, only to grab their prize and run off into the dust. The cloud of gritty happiness instantly turned into a nightmare before our eyes. Our plan was to help, to give back. I guess on some unconscious level, to feel special. Maybe even to stroke our egos, I don't know. Oh, and how it backfired! I felt completely sick to my stomach. These kids were now beating each other up in front of us, all because of our naïve actions.

We hadn't thought it through. Or at least, I know I hadn't. And it felt absolutely horrible. I struggled through the rest of that hike, just wanting to sit on a rock and cry. It hurt my heart that my actions had resulted in such unintended consequences. Instead of joy, I had sown strife. It was a painful lesson in cognitive thought. There are no easy answers in this life. For me, I just had to know that I could only do my best with what I knew in that moment. Once I knew better, I would do better. Ask questions. Dig deep for information. Make sure that my intentions do not stem from my ego. Once again, I'm a work in progress… That scene of good intentions gone wrong will always be fresh in my memory.

> *"One cannot resist the lure of Africa."*
> *–Rudyard Kipling*

The Ngorongoro Crater is the Earth's largest, intact, inactive volcanic crater and is home to a plethora of African wildlife.
Just south of the well-known Serengeti, the Ngorongoro Crater is a much smaller version of a natural wildlife area. But it also houses what is commonly called the Big Five in African terms.

Big game outfitters coined this term to describe the five most difficult animals to hunt in the bush. The Big Five were lion, leopard, bush elephant, cape buffalo, and black rhinoceros. They brought in the safari money, along with the thrill of the sightings. The Ngorongoro Crater had them all, including the lesser animals to the big stars, which were necessary to a healthy ecosystem, if not compulsory for a robust tourist economy!

I had planned to go to the Serengeti on safari. However, I lacked the proper travel visa and was denied entry into Kenya. Consequently, I was forced to turn back south through Tanzania. I was "stuck" with the Crater. Sometimes the path less traveled lends to a much more highly rewarding experience, as was the case here. And, as with my sailing adventure in Australia, the Universe knew better than I what my plan should be.

And again, the two of us, Pippa and I, signed up for a three-day Land Rover camping trip into the Crater. For a backpacker, it was one of those rare splurges that can set you back financially for weeks, but there is no way around it. It's a once-in-a-lifetime shot and you can't turn it down simply because of money (yes, this is privilege speaking). We sucked up the hit to the wallet and signed onto the safari, which bought us three days of absolute wonder, amazement, culinary delights, secure enclosed camping in the middle of the bush, and a tour guide to do all the work for us. Pretty cool and vastly appreciated for it was indeed a once-in-a-lifetime experience – money well spent!

It was just as you would expect to see on a National Geographic special, except I was in it! There were four of us in the Land Rover, a guide/driver, and a cook/camp host. Pippa and I, along with the other couple sharing our amazing adventure, were spoiled by having our big, canvas tent set up for us both nights, in fenced-in, secured areas out in the middle of the bush where we fell asleep and woke up to the sounds of the wildlife that surrounded us. It was a bit disconcerting, yet quite exhilarating, to fall asleep in a tent, to the sound of lions roaring, hyenas cackling, and baboons calling back and forth to each other.

Envision, too, the complete lack of ambient light and the brilliance of the southern constellations, with which we were so unfamiliar, dazzling our eyes away from above, so clear and magnificent. The culinary skills of the camp host/chef were extraordinary; he fed us outstandingly excellent meals for both breakfast and dinner in camp, and a bagged lunch to be enjoyed while out in the field in the Land Rover. The vehicle itself was just what you would see in the movies, all open aired on the sides and totally amped up to handle the rough, off-road terrain we were traversing.

But the animals stole the show, of course. During the day, the prides of lions resting themselves in the shade of trees and bushes, rolling around lazily in the dirt, and basically just looking regal and God-like, in general. There were eight prides of lions in the Crater, the most studied lions in the world. Water buffalos, although seemingly huge, slow, lazy looking creatures, are actually among the most dangerous in Africa. Their nasty dispositions, immense size, and menacing horns can and will do damage to anything that sets them off. They also make some very curious and disgusting noises! We were fortunate enough to behold the beauty and elegance of one black rhino, which we were told was also a formidable foe. Then there were the elephants, OH, the elephants!! Seemingly hundreds of them, from huge to just little babies.

To say we were awe-struck would have been an understatement. We were thoroughly enchanted by the elephants. These enormous creatures exuded such a calm, loving energy, we had to be admonished to stay in the vehicle multiple times. We all just wanted to stroke their wizened, crepe-like skin. We were able to get close enough to some of them that we could actually see into their eyes. It was like staring into the soul of a loving, compassionate, misunderstood giant. How could something so large, with the capacity for complete destruction, feel so loving and gentle? It was simply an amazing scene and energy to experience, and I believe we all felt utterly humbled in their magnificent presence. How could we not?

It was while we were having our "moment" with these seemingly gentle giants that both Pippa and I heard our names being called from out there in the bush somewhere. It was like being pulled out of a daze, quite confusing and disconcerting. Looking around, we realized it was Derek, our Silverback, calling to us from a nearby Land Rover. Derek!! Right there in front of us! Immediately, I opened the door and started to get out to run to his Land Rover and give him a huge hug. Luckily my ever-present guide pulled me back into my seat.

"What are you DOING?! DO NOT LEAVE THIS VEHICLE!" was my scolding.

Oh, right, we were surrounded by wild African elephants… Oops! Derek was in the next vehicle laughing his ass off at me. Our driver and his driver did eventually meander away from the herd of elephants so we could all share in our surprise and ecstatic reunion. Turns out our Silverback decided to go on safari after his gorilla experience, and there he was, right in front of us! Surreal and completely serendipitous. Pippa and I were overjoyed by this surprise turn of events. What are the odds of running into a close friend while on a safari in the middle of a pack of elephants in the remote African bush? Ah, the Universe definitely has a sense of humor, a flair for the dramatic, and keen radar to reconnect kindred souls.

Once I had experienced the magic and splendor of safari and witnessed incidents of the natural cycle of life and death in the wilderness, I found it impossible to ignore the ominous presence of poachers. How could they kill these animals? Why? For what? The notion was absolutely barbaric to me. That anyone could focus, point, and shoot a weapon at these wild, magnificent, innocent creatures was completely beyond my capacity of understanding. Even the predator animals were innocent of the ways of human cruelty. They killed for survival, not to inflict pain or be cruel or to get rich.

Early in my African adventure, a few of us from a hostel went for a sunrise hike on the open savannah. We were warned by our guide, which was mandatory through the national park, about running into poachers. A sunrise hike would coincide directly in timeframe with the poachers' return from a night at work. And, in fact, we did run into a group of men in dark clothing, with rifles slung across their shoulders, walking in the opposite direction from us.

We were warned to not make direct eye contact with them. Just lower our heads and let them walk past. How? How could we just pretend we didn't see them? How could we not want to use their own weapons against them? How could we not face brutality with brutality? Well, in this instance, the guide explained that the organizations that fight poaching in that area were doing the best with what they had. But it wasn't enough. They needed more people. They needed more money. They needed more weapons.

"More than what?" I wanted to know. The answer was, more than the poachers. But there were more of them than the good guys. And it was about money. Lots of money. More money than a simple life or two was worth. And we had to be careful because we were those lives, as well as the animals they preyed upon. No eye contact if we wanted to come back alive from that sunrise hike.

But we all came back with questions and feelings of injustice. It was all ridiculously unfair. As with so many other times, there were no simple answers. Money, violence, greed, power… Unfortunately, these factors seemed to rule the African world, and that included the wildlife. It was simply part of the reality there, as it still seems to be now.

Towards the end of my African adventure, Pippa and I found ourselves camped out at a huge campsite near Victoria Falls in Zimbabwe. Derek had made his way down to join us for a few nights, and it was fantastic to be together again. It was my last stop before heading down to Cape Town to catch my flight back to the States, and I was doing everything in my power to make it last as long as possible.

One of those afternoons, Derek decided he was going to seize the opportunity to fling his body off the bridge over Vic Falls – as they're called there. I couldn't conjure up the nerve to actually go bungee jumping, so I stood on the platform with him as his support system. I'm really not crazy about heights, so actually jumping myself was quite out of the question. But I will admit that the view from that platform was world-class exquisite! Victoria Falls is the waterway that divides Zimbabwe from South Africa, and in high water season it's not just one waterfall, it's mile after mile of waterfalls.

The Zambezi River – yes, the river I did not raft – drops almost 400 feet from one series of cascading falls to the lower plateau beneath. It was not quite high-water season for Derek's plunge. Still, the scene was unforgettable. Derek, standing at the top of that bridge with his feet tied to a very long bungee cord, and behind him, illuminating him, the rainbow that forms at all hours from the mist of the Falls. It was absolutely stunning. He was crazy; it was stupid high, and it was completely breathtaking. I'm pretty sure I was very little comfort to him before he jumped off the 400-foothigh bridge to the roiling waters below. And I'm also pretty sure that my consolation was not the first thing on his mind at that moment. Just being a spectator, albeit at very close quarters, was more than enough of an adrenaline rush for me.

Crazy bugger!

During our few days at that campsite, I had to just push my limits one more time. On the main bulletin board, which held all kinds of notes and memos for people, kind of like a backpacker's version of classified ads, I found a post from a few guys traveling in a Land

Rover who were looking for another two travelers to go through the Okavango Delta with them.

If you haven't heard of the Okavango Delta before, it is just barely one step down in popularity from the Serengeti. Although, it has a slightly higher appeal for those who are more the do-it-yourselfers than the higher-end safari tours. This was exactly that opportunity. It would be four of us in their personal Land Rover, trekking off through one of the most remote and lusted after places on Earth.

Of course, Pippa and I met with the Land Rover fellas and talked about possibilities, and we were offered the spots on the excursion. But I was in a bit of a predicament... Well over a month ago I made that infamous three-minute phone call to my mom in New Jersey under the premise of needing money to get down to South Africa to catch my flight out. But here I was, still in Africa, obviously in no hurry to catch a plane back to the States.

If I were to accept a seat on this Okavango Delta trek, I would have to change my flight, yet again, in order to make it happen. And the only person on the planet who could help me coordinate all those flight changes was my mother. Well, fuck... Even I, being the most self-absorbed daughter on the face of the planet, couldn't do that to her. Again. But... It was the Okavango Delta!! I mean, Jesus... That was a hard one, having to turn that opportunity down. But I just couldn't do it. It was almost like the Universe was testing my limits. And, GOD, was that a challenge! What a crazy, exciting opportunity to have on my plate. To this day, almost thirty years later, I have very few regrets in life, but passing that up is one of them. I arrived in Cape Town just a few days later.

> *"The eye never forgets what the heart has seen."*
> *–Bantu proverb*

It was one of the hardest parts of my African adventure, witnessing such rampant injustice. It was everywhere. Infused in the prides of lions on the savannahs, lurking in the dirt streets of the local villages, woven into the patterns of almost every living thing on the continent. Injustice. And it didn't seem to be going anywhere anytime soon.

It was, and still is, the unfortunate hand that has been dealt to Africa for so many centuries. The dichotomy of the local children laughing, singing, and dancing in the dirt streets while streams of sewage and trash passed underfoot mirrored the divide between soul and circumstance.

And what about the villagers drumming the sun into the sacred new day while sitting in a dilapidated shack made of mud, surrounded by machinegun-slinging zealots? In fact, it is these contradictions, these stark realities that make Africa, Africa. The resilience of a people who have undergone staggering poverty, massive disease, and macabre genocide is beyond astonishing. It is hope. Pure and simple. And with that hope, there is pure beauty. The beauty of the people, the wildlife, the landscape… This juxtaposition of injustice and pure beauty was the magic that I found there.

> *"As soon as you trust yourself, you will know how to live."*
> –Goethe

As fate would have it, Derek and I met up sporadically for a few years after that trip to continue our adventures on smaller scales. Also, as fate would have it, we never did move our friendship from platonic friends to lovers. Our bond was on a level of special that simply couldn't be challenged like that! Sometimes you just don't fuck with a good thing.

There was that one time he traveled to the States with his friend, Ben, bought a big traveling van we called Bertha, and the three of us took a road trip from Colorado to Mexico. We camped on the beach, drank margaritas, waited around in a little coastal town for a week or so before the shrimp arrived for The Festival de Camerón. I believe it was that trip the three of us ended up climbing rocks in the desert at

Joshua Tree National Park, as well as camping out in Yellowstone National Park.

And, of course, he also popped up in Alaska at one point and spent some time exploring Homer and the Kenai Peninsula where I was living with Josh (my park ranger boyfriend of many years). Those impromptu visits and trips happened for a while before he decided that he had found his woman and went back to Australia to settle down.

Although Pippa and I never did meet up again in person after our Africa adventures, we have maintained our connection She ended up back in the UK, married, and had twins. To this day, almost three decades later, all three of us still manage to keep in touch via social media. All of our paths leading in such different directions over the years…

My broken heart was fortunate enough to get quite the jump start to mending after those three months in Africa, including from a most unexpected source. Before I departed, I did get to see him again, and he was still a mess about the whole thing. One of us had to make up his mind, and I sure as hell wasn't going to wait around for him to bump me to second best. Ironically, I spent the day with his mother right before I left, and I remember her wise words to me:

"It would never work between you two. You are way too strong and independent of a woman for my son. He needs to be needed." Those words got me through many more phases of my broken heart. And, indeed, he chose the woman with many more needs than I. Although, in the span of things, our two-year relationship doesn't seem to be enough time to do any kind of serious damage, it destroyed me on so many levels of intimacy. A clairvoyant once told me that, in a previous life, he had bought me as a mail-order bride from a poverty-stricken situation, and when I arrived, he refused me and I died in the streets due to his abandonment.

    I'm not really sure how much weight I put on something like that, but it sure as hell has made a lot of sense out of a shitty situation. As I noted before, dozens of men within the next twenty-five years of my life were left, literally left, confused in a wake of suppressed abandonment and intimacy issues.

    There were some close calls in that time, but ultimately, my heart wouldn't allow me to seriously commit to anyone for decades after Warren. I can proudly announce that I am now married and living happily with the one man who seems, miraculously, able to keep me around. As one of my friends once said, "catching you is like catching a twenty-pound fish on a six-pound line." Well said. And, yes, my husband can fish.

    After all was said and done, I can now say, "Thank you, Warren." If it weren't for him, at the very least, I wouldn't have had such amazing adventures in Africa. At the most, maybe I would have married the wrong man. Who knows? But I do know that I am grateful for his role in my life, though it took a while to reach that place in my head and in my heart.

That year was epic! Six months in Australia, followed closely by another three months in Africa, primed me for so many more adventures in life. Those experiences helped mold me into the woman I was to become, the woman I am. I was too young and naïve at the time to realize how important that time was for me. It enabled me to grow into my strength and independence.

My future move to rural Alaska, followed by a twenty-five-year stretch as an entrepreneur, chef, and restaurant owner, was possible because of the confidence and resilience I nurtured during that year abroad. I listened to my intuition and followed it to the far-off reaches of the planet, and along the way I learned myself.

Yes, I learned myself. I got to know what I was made of. And I was able to build on that core to birth a future me I was – and am – truly proud of (most of the time, anyway). My life motto has become, "Nothing is impossible. Maybe highly improbable, but not impossible." And my pal Goethe also said, "Magic is believing in yourself; if you can do that, you can make anything happen."

After all was said and done, my flight from Cape Town ended in Philadelphia, where my mother was kind enough to pick me up. After spotting her car among the many parked at the curb outside of the baggage claim, I headed her way with my dirty, beat-up backpack strapped to my back. I certainly didn't fit in with the glossy business travelers and recently returned, refreshed, vacationers milling about. After a welcome hug, she looked me up and down with disapproving eyes and made one of the most ridiculous comments I could ever have imagined upon returning from my recent overseas exploits.

"Honey, you don't match," motioning to my worse-for-wear hippie skirt and floral printed shirt.

"Really, Mom?"

"Nothing is impossible. Maybe highly improbable, but not impossible."
-Lisa Ruoff

Lisa Ruoff

After Thoughts

"Only when it is dark enough, can you see the stars."
-Martin Luther King

In the writing of this memoir, decades after the actual experiences, I am overcome with rumination. While I was traveling, it was for the sake of living in the moment and being open to the next magical encounter. Twenty-five years later, I realize how absolutely blessed I was to have been in the presence of such beauty, wonder, and adventure. Times change. The world moves on. Unfortunately, sometimes it moves in a less than positive and life-affirming direction.

I don't mean to become a cliché and go all "rogue hippie" on you. But this is my book and these are my After Thoughts. If you're not in the mood for a dose of reality based on my experiences, or a bit of Buddhist perspective, then now is the time to put the book down. But, as the saying goes, the light does not exist without the dark.

When I was young and traveling, I didn't fully understand how utterly privileged I was. The sights, sounds, people, and places were (mostly) beautiful, always amazing, and I was grateful, yes. But as the years have passed, the darkness has shown itself. The gross injustice of poverty and sickness. The decline of the penguin colonies, or the eradication of the gorillas in the Congo. Yet, at the same time my heart aches due to witnessing the darkness, I am simultaneously awe-struck that I had the opportunity to partake of it all in the first place. Ah, the dance of dark and light…

    The Great Barrier Reef (GRB) is one of the Seven Wonders of the Natural World and a United Nations World Heritage site. It is longer than the Great Wall of. China, stretching 1,400 miles. The GRB is the only living thing visible from outer space. It is comprised of billions of tiny living organisms known as coral polyps. The reef is home also to a tremendous diversity of wildlife: thirty species of whale, 1,500 species of fish, six species of turtle that come to lay their eggs, 215 species of birds, and so many others. Many of these species are considered vulnerable or endangered.

    While snorkeling on the Great Barrier Reef, I was absolutely unaware that in my lifetime this amazing ecosystem would falter to the brink of collapse. In 1995 coral bleaching was just emerging as an area of research. Yes, the sea temperatures were rising, but only the thought of mass destruction of such beauty and diversity was a possibility. I had no idea that within a few decades – not even a half of a lifetime - the categorical death of an ecosystem of such epic proportion could even be a possibility.

Coral bleaching has caused such utter devastation to the reef systems of the world, including the Great Barrier Reef, that what I was fortunate enough to partake of is no longer an option. It may never be seen as the wonderous, beautiful, symbiotic ecosystem that it was in 1995. It's quite the dichotomy, to be so honored and blessed to have experienced such an amazing life force, while feeling simultaneously sick to know that we, as a species, have destroyed a living masterpiece beyond recognition and repair.

Then again, in the view of Buddhism, there is no good or bad, right or wrong. Everything just IS. Suffering is only something we conceive of intellectually, not in actuality. Coral bleaching and the death of an ecosystem could be viewed simply as another instance in the cycle of life or the passage of time (the latter of which is also an illusion, but we won't get into that right now!). It's all just part of the process. Maybe… But my heart still aches over it. It still causes me great grief to witness such "change" and not see irrefutable death and destruction.

In the time that has passed from 1995 to 2023, so much has changed that I wouldn't be able to tell the same story as I've just written. The Great Barrier Reef, along with almost 80% of reef systems in the world, have been so distressed by coral bleaching that they are on the brink of complete collapse. Another side effect of warming oceans is the lack of food for the fairy penguins that mom and I went to witness in Australia. They have to swim farther and farther out to sea to find food and due to this, their numbers are also dwindling.

The beloved gorillas Derek, our own "Silverback," visited in Congo are critically endangered due to choices made by humans. Decisions driven mostly by greed over resources in habitat areas that lie above the oil and gas deposits. The oil and gas industry is not empathetic to the utter destruction and death they leave behind. Corporate leadership, buttressed by strategic media campaigns to garner public support or mitigate dissent, consider habitat destruction and death of species acceptable collateral damage for what they consider the greater good. Their influence extends beyond their boardrooms to politicians and banks and the list goes on.

Poaching and human sprawl have taken their toll on more than the gorilla populations in Africa. As of December 2022, there are only two white rhinos left in existence, and they are both female. The future isn't looking good for them. The African elephant population is, along with the gorillas, critically endangered. As Dr Bruno Oberle, IUCN (International Union for the Conservation of Nature) Director General says, "We must urgently put an end to poaching and ensure that sufficient suitable habitat for both forest and savanna elephants is conserved." Both ivory poaching and loss of habitat are direct effects of human actions. Even the little island of Tasmania is not immune to the darkness. The Tasmanian devil population has declined by over 90% in the past twenty years, rendering it an endangered species. As of 2022, there were only 25,000 left in the wild on the island, down from over 150,000 in 1996. They've been absent from the mainland until recently. They are the only carnivorous marsupial in the world. And contrary to popular belief, they are small, approximately two feet in length and weighing between 13 and 16 pounds. A highly infectious cancer, Devil Facial Tumor Disease (DFTD), is the primary culprit of their decimation The cancer currently has no cure.

But there is light attempting to penetrate the darkness. The Tasmanian devil population has not lived on the mainland of Australia for over 3,000 years, largely due to the introduction of dingoes, Australia's wild dog. There is a program dedicated to reviving the Tasmanian devil population. Nine devils were born in captivity early in 2022, raising hopes for a successful breeding program that will lead to introduction of the mainland born Tassie devils to the wild. Many more babies need to be born and survive. Before any are introduced to Tasmania, a cure must be found for the cancer.

These facts are quite overwhelming. I've shared only those most relevant to my travels. The world is changing.

More specifically, we are changing the world. Once again, from a Buddhist perspective, there is no right or wrong – good or bad. But, also, according to Buddha, simplicity is essential. Live simply so that others may simply live. Not just humans, but others. All others. Gorillas, elephants, Tasmanian devils, fairy penguins, coral reefs… What, in our minds, makes a gorilla or a penguin any less worthy than a human? Are we really that cold and heartless as a species? Or is it all subconscious? How did we become so disconnected from everything and each other? We are completely unaware of the cause and effect of our actions. We have created a world that is quickly becoming dystopian.

> *"If you do not change direction, you will end up where you are going."* -Buddhist Proverb

While I do not call myself a Buddhist, certain Buddhist beliefs comfort me. They give me hope. As social, economic, and political pressures mount across the globe, and with them attendant social unrest and violence, perhaps more people will be drawn to Buddhist principles of co-existence, peace, simplicity, and harmony. I will do my best to promote these principles, largely by living them. My fervent prayer is that more people will be drawn to Buddha's example and there may yet be hope for humanity. . .

Lisa Ruoff

Dedication

First and foremost, although I doubt he will ever know, I thank Warren for breaking up with me. That occurrence set into motion one of the biggest and best adventures of my life, and I am eternally grateful for my African experience. Without knowing it, or meaning to, in that one decision, he shaped a part of me that will never be the same again. Another huge thanks goes out to my mother. I'm glad you made the mistake of getting pregnant with me! And, of course, my extremely loving, understanding, and motivating husband, Jay. A huge thanks to him for not taking any of my past relationships as a threat, and more so, being my biggest fan (according to him!). He is my rock. The yang to my yin. I am so lucky to have found him. Even though it was a bit of a rough ride because it took much, much longer than anticipated to turn things around, my editor, Carolyn, is owed a huge thanks for doing an excellent job. I appreciate it more than you know, my dear! Of course, all of you strong, independent women out there – keep on pushing buttons and being intimidating (are they intimidated or are you intimidating them?)! The world needs you! On a broader spectrum, I give huge thanks to all of those out there who give something of themselves for the betterment of others and the planet. It's going to take all of us to make some kind of a shift into the light. And a big thanks for Pippa and Derek for being there to share in the adventure. After 25 years, each of you remains a part of my heart.

To everyone who has lent a hand along my path, I thank you. There are way too many people that have offered help or support along the way for my memory to keep up with or my pen to do them justice. Life is good but it is so much better with loving energy from friends and family!

And I am full of gratitude.

— — — — — — — — — — — — — — — — —

www.ingramcontent.com/pod-product-compliance
Lightning Source LLC
Chambersburg PA
CBHW071437080526
44587CB00014B/1881